The Job Hunter's *Spiritual* Companion

by William Carver

Innisfree
Press, Inc.

*A call to the
deep heart's core*

Innisfree Press, Inc.
136 Roumfort Road
Philadelphia, PA 19119-1632

Cover design by Hugh Duffy.

Library of Congress Cataloging-in-Publication Data
    Carver, William, date.
        The job hunter's spiritual companion / by William
        Carver.
            p.   cm.
        Includes bibliographical references.
        ISBN 1-880913-30-5
        1. Vocation—Meditations.   2. Unemployed —
    Prayer–books and devotions—English.   3. Devotional
    calendars. I. Title.
    BL629.C37   1998   97-44678
    248.8'6—dc21   CIP

To Will, my shining light on the Journey.

*To Christina, Elizabeth, and Catherine,
with gratitude for your love
as we walk the path together.*

Contents

Acknowledgments

One thing I know: At its center, this book was a gift to me from the Universe. In a real sense, I have benefited immensely from it, and I give thanks to God for this opportunity.

Many people have contributed to this work. As you might suspect, they are far too numerous to mention. That my family contributed significantly almost goes without saying, but I want to be certain that they know I recognize and deeply value their help.

A few people who made contributions to this particular work are especially worthy of note. They are, in no particular order, Paulette Smith, Randall Stone, Guy Brewer, Rick Starkweather, Sharon Hoover, John Hoover, Judd Shaw, Mike Hopkins, Susan Stone, Al Bonnyman, Maxine Rosen, Ed Smith, Connie Adams, Dennis Adams, Curtis Parham, and Marcia Broucek; and Charlie, Stacy, Mark and John of Wilderness River Adventures, Page, Arizona.

Special thanks to Carolyn Perry Bryant, who had the courage to take a chance and give a young man a start on this journey.

I rejoice that I am able to share this gift with you. Receive it in Love.

Prologue

I am sitting in the back seat of a Saab that smells of new plastic and leather. To my left are my friend Susan and her husband, Randall. The rest of the car is filled with Susan's boss's family. It is a warm autumn day in Williamsburg, Virginia, in September of 1989. We are on our way to a William and Mary football game, and I am trying desperately to get fired up, to get in the spirit.

All I feel is fear.

In less than two weeks, I will be starting a job I just accepted in Richmond. Though the job sounds okay, I seem to have made a shambles of everything else in my life. My marriage is teetering on the edge of divorce, and I am emotionally wrecked.

All that time searching for a job . . .
Have I made the right decision?

I'm sure the new job will work out just fine . . .
But maybe taking this job was a mistake . . .
Starting my own business might have been better . . .
But, then again, a new business would never make it . . .
Perhaps I should go back home . . .
No, I need to stay here . . .

I know I have a purpose,
but it's hard to see at the moment . . .

I feel confused and afraid.

Why am I here?

The Place to Start

There is work with your name on it. I truly believe that. You have a reason for being here, a sacred purpose that is trying to find you.

I want to assist you in connecting with your own spiritual depths — as well as the spiritual current that runs through all creation — in the context of your career and your life's work, your purpose. I may offer some practical job hunting tips along the way, but I am more interested in cultivating a profound and radical openness to the life of the spirit, to your ultimate purpose.

There are many paths to career success. What you need to know — and believe — is that you already have everything you need to be successful within your unique purpose. You need not be afraid. If you lose your way along the path occasionally, that's okay. The spiritual approach, in many ways like the scientific approach, is self-correcting. By cultivating the spiritual disciplines, you will learn the value of the lessons along the way.

In these next pages, I propose we journey together: I will help you get in touch with your purpose — with that peaceful place within that tells you that you belong, that you are doing what you came here to do. Your part of the journey is to give yourself fully to the process, to commit to the success of living out your unique purpose. I believe the way will be made clear. If you need to, borrow my belief for a while, until your own belief is stronger.

The Job Hunter's Spiritual Companion is a supplement to other job search or career development resources you may be using. There are many good ones out there, and you can read brief summaries of some of them in the Bibliography. This is not intended to replace any of them: This is not a "how to" book but, rather, a "how to think about it" book.

I urge you not to rush through these pages. This book is short, and, I hope, easy for you to read and comprehend. But, please, do not get in a hurry: The ideas are meant to be considered, regarded, lingered over. Allow the concepts to soak into your consciousness and your being.

As an act of love and kindness toward yourself, promise to do the work necessary for the living out of your purpose. You have been freely given the great power of thought, the great power of your mind. You can choose now to put this power to work for your own benefit.

Try this: Instead of thinking about job hunting as something difficult to be endured, think of it as the *IDEAL* time to re-examine your skills, strengths, and interests that will point you to your sacred purpose in life.

Today's Spiritual Guideline

For each step of this process, I want to offer you a chance to go deeper, to get in touch with a larger Universe than your daily job search. Each section concludes with *Today's Spiritual Guideline* that I hope will open some doors for you to new perspectives and renewed belief in yourself. Although I have written these to be used in the mornings, before you begin your day, feel free to adjust the timing and usage to fit your needs. For some, the sequence of reflections and spiritual guidelines I have laid out will be helpful. For others, a different sequence may be more immediately helpful. Select what fits your needs.

I recommend that you start by selecting a journal or notebook to use for keeping a record of your thoughts, ideas, and feelings as we take this journey together.

For your first entry, write a letter to yourself (or to an imaginary mentor or wisdom figure, if that seems more helpful), describing your commitment to finding your sacred purpose in life. Include what scares you about the journey and what excites you.

2 *There Is a Reason*

Deep inside you, there is a knowing: There is a reason you came into being at this time and place. The paradox is that what seems to be a random event in a random Universe is, in fact, purposeful. At the very core of your being, you may want to trust this, but sometimes it's difficult to translate that knowledge into practical, manageable, daily-life terms. In other words, you may have a sense of a grand design and purpose in your life, but you're just not sure how to put it into practice.

Part of the problem is our work ethic. We've been taught that, in order to accomplish something worthwhile, we have to work *really* hard at it — and that usually implies no pleasure, no fun, no excitement, only hard work. Yet, philosophically, I believe that the fulfillment of our purpose on this planet can be joyful. In fact, it *must* be joyful. By definition, if what we are doing is a constant struggle or drudgery, the Universe is sending us a very important message: *Don't* do that. That is not the reason you are here.

The goal of this book is to offer you some tools for an effective spiritual approach to finding the reason you are here.

In preparation for this work, I drift back in my mind to the day I described in the *Prologue*, that day in Williamsburg when I was feeling scared, upset, and directionless. Thinking I had created a disaster and making it worse by continually grappling with it. Trying to analyze my failures but not learning from them — in actual fact, setting myself up for more of them. Looking back on the tapestry of events that followed, I can see how my life's purpose began to evolve, to become clearer. We salvaged our marriage, brought two more beautiful children into the world, and I began the process of making peace with God and the world, of finding my connection to God and the Universe, to the flow of life.

I will help you pursue and love this search for the discovery and living of your sacred purpose. Here's a secret: Pay attention to your *intention* to bring your purpose into the light of reality.

Today's Spiritual Guideline

In your journal, make a list of obstacles that seem in the way of finding your purpose.

Then consider and write down any signs or reasons you can think of why this might be the *best* time to seek out your purpose in life.

Conclude by reaffirming, in writing, your intention to seek out your reason for being here.

3 Twelve Considerations

As you embark upon the task of infusing spirituality and the sacred into your job search, I want to suggest twelve principles for your consideration. I urge you not to skip across them lightly. Think about each one in its turn and allow the full meaning of each concept to enter the depths of your being.

1. I have a sacred purpose for being upon the Earth at this time and in this place.

2. I have everything I need for my purpose in life.

3. The foundation for my spiritual search is a daily, fundamental openness to the lessons that are continuously being presented to me.

4. It may be necessary to create a radical break from my routine, from the way I have always done things.

5. I will embrace and welcome uncertainty, ambiguity — even failure — into my life, knowing that the seemingly chaotic is the ground of all creation.

6. Things are not always what they appear to be; life is an ever-changing kaleidoscope.

7. The Creator and the created are inseparably linked.

8. I will look for the places of humor in my life and remind myself to enjoy the comedy.

9. I will listen to the wisdom that is within me.

10. I will listen to the wisdom that is around me.

11. I will be open to the lessons and opportunities in life's paradoxes.

12. I will follow my heart.

Today's Spiritual Guideline

Select two different colored pens or pencils for your writing today.

In one color, copy in your journal any of these twelve considerations that particularly attract you.

In another color, copy any of the considerations that seem difficult.

Write about your thoughts and feelings in response to the considerations you have selected.

4 — Twelve Practical Steps

In conducting any job or career search, there are certain fundamental steps you need to follow. The spiritual foundation of each of these steps will be presented as you go through this book. For now, read the list of steps carefully, taking mental note of which steps you have already taken and which steps are ahead of you. Even if some of these steps seem "old" to you in your job search process, remind yourself that your new focus on your spiritual life will infuse these activities with new meaning.

1. Start with a well-articulated objective.

2. Know your desired physical location.

3. Know yourself — your skills, abilities, strengths, and preferences.

4. Develop a résumé that will "sell" your mission to those who see it.

5. Invest time in getting to know *people,* not just markets, companies, and opportunities.

6. Build a network of relationships, starting with where you are: friends, acquaintances, and business associates. Ask for what you really need: information, guidance, wisdom, assistance, assurance.

7. Be willing to refine your objective and direction in the process; be open to learning what each step of the process has to teach you.

8. Record and document your process: information received, referrals, letters, leads. Organize your files in a system that works for you.

9. Identify and seek out allies who can assist you along the path.

10. Before you respond to any ad or recruiter, carefully consider how the job fits with your mission and purpose.

11. When it comes time to interview, think circular: prepare, follow-up, thank, persist.

12. Negotiate for your legitimate needs, for what you need to live out your purpose in the physical dimension.

Today's Spiritual Guideline

Re-read the letter you wrote at the outset of your journal.

With your commitment to finding your sacred purpose fresh in your mind, choose one of these twelve practical steps to focus on today. Copy it into your journal.

Write your thoughts about how you might take some action on this step in the next twenty-four hours with a new openness.

5   *A Spiritual Practice*

There are many ways, such as meditation, prayer, or a moment of silence, to get more in touch with your spiritual dimension. There are also many spiritual advisors who can assist you in this quest. Be open to their appearance in your life.

To help you integrate your spiritual life with your job search, I recommend engaging in a committed, daily spiritual practice, combining meditation and prayer. Think of it as giving yourself a loving discipline during which you will pay attention to your inner spiritual life.

During the period of your job search, when you are considering so many issues, I think it is particularly important to set aside three specific times each day for a spiritual practice of some kind. I've outlined three possible practices for you to consider. Use what fits for you and supplement as you choose with other personal, spiritual, and religious practices.

I will tell you this: If you are faithful to a spiritual practice, you will stay on the path to find what you are seeking. Your spiritual practice, however you design it, will become a rich source of meaning and direction for your vocation, your work, and your entire life.

ON RISING:

When you first awake, give thanks for this day and all it represents.

Become silent, focusing only on your breathing. Remain silent for approximately three minutes.

Petition, either silently or aloud, to be shown direction this day, to give and receive assistance, and to be brought into contact with the people you need, who also need you.

Visualize beginning the day prepared both spiritually and physically for the challenges ahead.

Consider that this day you will participate in the act of creation together with the Creator.

Affirm to yourself that you belong where you are and that you have a purpose for being.

AT MID-DAY OR EARLY EVENING:
Give thanks for the gift of the day, whatever it is bringing you.
Sit in silence for three minutes, concentrating on your breathing.
Let your mind empty of the day's concerns.
Present petitions:
- for continuing guidance
- for direction
- for peace
- for happiness
- for humor
- for prosperity
- for work you love
- for a geographic location that fits you
- for mutually rewarding relationships
- for the ability to give freely
- for the ability to receive freely
- for the happiness of family
- for the happiness of friends
- for any other needs

Visualize receiving what you need.
Vow to be open to all forms of the "answers."
End by quietly giving thanks.

AT BEDTIME:
Give thanks for the experience of this day.
Enter a silent, meditative state.
Read:
- from a sacred text
- from a spiritual work
- from a book of meditations
- from other books that have touched you, or that have been offered you by friends or spiritual advisors

After your reading, be still and open to the revelations for at least five minutes, allowing the reading to permeate your spirit.
Consider how you might put revelations from your reading into practice in the coming day.

Give thanks for any events of the day that seemed particularly helpful; give thanks for events that seemed particularly hard.

Re-affirm that you have lived a good day upon this Earth.

Today's Spiritual Guideline

Make a commitment to yourself that you will start a discipline of spiritual practice. Decide how, when, and where you will engage in your practice.

Write in your journal a statement of your commitment and your plan for implementing your spiritual practice.

6 *"I Need a Job"*

People come to me every day looking for work.
I ask them, "What is your objective?"

Their answers are often nonspecific, fuzzy, or indefinite. Sometimes they simply don't know.

"I just need a job . . . Something that pays well . . . Something to do while I'm going to school . . . Something to get me out of the house. I'm going stir crazy . . . It really doesn't matter. Anything's got to be better than what I've been doing."

In point of fact, it *does* matter.

Every single one of us has a purpose for being here. I know that with every fiber of my being. In my experience as a human resources professional and career consultant, I have found that truly content people know and are in touch with and are living out their purpose.

Why then, at times, does the way seem so muddled?

I think we cause ourselves much heartache in this area. Messages are streaming into us from early childhood telling us what we "should" want. This is not to say that any particular wants, desires, careers, or professions are right or wrong. It is to say that purpose is unique to each individual.

Part of the answer is to begin and continue a process of learning about yourself, of learning to *be* yourself.

Today's Spiritual Guideline

Assuming that you have completed at least one day of your personal spiritual practice, record how you felt at the conclusion of this day. What did you notice about yourself — your feelings, your physical reactions, your thoughts? What did you learn? Write your observations in your journal.

7   Crossing the Desert

"Desert Experiences" can take many forms: the challenge of unemployment; the daily grind of a job you find loathsome; a prolonged spiritual, physical, or financial difficulty. When you feel alone in the desert, it is easy to become depressed, angry, stressed, and worried, and to take on the behaviors of a chronic complainer.

There is another way.

Many spiritual leaders, including Moses and Jesus and Mother Teresa, have utilized the Desert Experience as a means of reflection, prayer, meditation, clarification, strengthening, and defining the particular mission at hand. Opening yourself to the experience opens a new way to cross your particular desert.

Start by fully acknowledging your feelings associated with your Desert Experience. Do not judge your feelings; simply let them in. Honor them. Embrace them as valued and welcome teachers.

Then quiet yourself and listen for what it is your emotions are telling you. Look for the possible lessons that might be available to you in the desert.

For example, if you find yourself in the position of being turned down for a job you wanted, you might realize that:

- This is not my path.
- I can grow and thrive in the face of adversity; I have the internal strength that I need.
- There are other people who need me and my special talents or insights.
- There is a mission for me that is not yet obvious.
- There are specific skills that I must learn in order to progress to my ultimate purpose.
- This Desert Experience is an opportunity for a time of quiet reflection into the nature and purpose of my work.
- This is a chance for me to challenge old beliefs that no longer work for me.
- There is another job more suited to me ahead.

Cultivate an openness to your special time in the desert.

Today's Spiritual Guideline

Think of an extended negative period that you have previously experienced in your life. It might include a health, financial, or relationship problem. Write a summary of that event or series of events in your journal.

Set your summary aside and go into a period of silence. Try not to dwell on your Desert Experience, but rather to allow only quiet to permeate your consciousness.

Then return to what you wrote. Consider thoughtfully any lessons that, in retrospect, you can see that came out of your Desert Experience.

Write in your journal some of the positive learnings and realizations from your previous desert crossing.

8 Intention

My intention is evident in what I have created.
Even if I don't immediately recognize it as my intention,
if I have created it, then it is so.

This is hard to accept.
I would like to give responsibility
for the situations in which I find myself —
particularly the negative situations —
to others:
>   my boss, my spouse, my parents, my children
>   my friends, my enemies, the President, the Pope
>   somebody else, anybody else.

Behold, my intention:
>   expressed in my job, my relationships
>   expressed in my financial picture, my mood
>   expressed in my weight, my physical condition
>   expressed in my daily experience.

If I don't pay attention to my intention,
my life can become a very slippery and puzzling affair.
An intention I didn't even know I had
will find a way to express itself.

What is at my very core?
And how do I make it real every day?
The doing — or not-doing —
always brings my intention into reality.

Today's Spiritual Guideline

Sit in a quiet space for at least five minutes. Ask yourself: *"What is my REAL intention? What am I really seeking out of a job or career?"* In your journal write a simple, straightforward statement of what you are seeking. For example, *"I am looking for a good paying job so that I can care for my family."*

Then ask yourself the question, *"Why?"* Record your answer. It might be something like this: *"Because it takes money to buy food."*

Continue asking the question *"Why?"* Go all the way back until you reach the fundamental reason for your behavior. For example:

- *"Because we need food to live, grow, and be happy."*
- *"Because I love my family, and I care about what happens to us."*
- *"Because loving and caring for people is a fundamental part of who I am."*

In this example, the core intention is to love and care for people. As you work with this exercise, you may find that you have several core intentions operating. Use this internal questioning process to help identify them.

9 *Responsibility*

I accept total responsibility for my situation.
No one else is in charge.
No one else is to blame.
I am responsible for
> this moment
> my job
> my financial status
> the way I live
> the way I care for others
> the success I am experiencing in my life
> my own happiness.

The responsibility is in my hands, every day.
If I put the power in the hands of others,
I make myself powerless.

If I agree within myself to accept sole responsibility
> for myself
> for everything in my life,

I can be for myself
and for others at the same time.

So, just for this day,
and this day alone,
I agree to be responsible
> for myself
> for all that I do
> for all that I think
> for all the meanings I assign.

My strength flows from this simple, radical choice —
to take responsibility for myself.

Today's Spiritual Guideline

Reflect on an incident that happened this week that you blamed (and may continue to blame) on someone else.

Write in your journal how you might have been at least partially responsible for what occurred. This is like opening a secret door, allowing yourself to get a glimpse of how you might have behaved differently, understanding what power you had in the situation that you did not own fully.

Jot down some possibilities of what you could change in the future that would contribute to a better outcome in such a situation.

10 Challenging Beliefs

Each of us comes into the job search — or any other adventure, for that matter — equipped with a set of beliefs about what we can and cannot accomplish, what we can and cannot do, what is possible and what is not.

At the core, these beliefs are simply that: beliefs — usually with a capital "B" because we often hold them so tightly. For a variety of reasons, we take great comfort in holding on to a set of beliefs that reinforce our concept of ourselves as limited beings. It is in the challenging of these beliefs within our spiritual being that we will be set free.

What are some of the beliefs you are carrying around? Being willing to look at them in the full light of day is the first step in taking away their power over you.

Do any of these sound familiar?

- I can't do that because I've never done it before.
- He's too busy and important. She'll never want to see me.
- Material prosperity is for someone else, not for me.
- I know where I would like my life to go, but it's just a pipe-dream. I need to get realistic and find a job that pays enough money and has good benefits.
- I could never get into that company. They wouldn't be interested in talking with me.
- I can't change careers now. That's just not reasonable or possible.
- I don't have enough education/training/experience for that job.
- This spiritual life business is fine for gurus and televangelists, but it just isn't practical for an average person like me on a job search.
- They might not like me, and I might not get the job. That would be a catastrophe.
- (Having gotten the job) They might not like me, and I might get fired. That would be a catastrophe.

- I'm alone. Nobody cares about me.
- As soon as I find the right job, everything in my life will be better. Then I/we will be happy.

The list is theoretically endless. These beliefs, and others like them, are daily lessons. If you actively challenge and thoroughly examine them, not only will you reap new learnings, but you will also be able to transcend these self-limiting beliefs.

Finding your purpose may involve *unlearning* what you have been told. You may need to peel away externally-imposed layers of expectation before you can know what you're really here to do.

Today's Spiritual Guideline

Select one of the beliefs from the above list — or any of your own self-limiting beliefs that you are aware of — and write it in your journal. Take a few minutes to write about ways that it holds you back.

Then write a belief statement that is the *opposite*.

Describe an imaginary job scenario for yourself if this opposite were true.

11 Complaining

What am I complaining about?

Sometimes, for no good reason I can discern,
I find myself complaining
about anything and everything
"It's their fault, not mine."
"How could they do such a thing?"
And so on.

Yet this complaining doesn't serve me.
Nor does it serve anyone else.
The complaining puts me into a frame of mind
where everything is wrong,
where nothing is right.

Complaining isolates and paralyzes me.
I may be "right,"
but because of all the negativity,
I block anything good from happening.

This complaining doesn't serve me,
so I will leave it behind now.
I ask forgiveness for wallowing in self-pity, and
I decide that this is not how I choose to live.

Today's Spiritual Guideline

Record all of your complaints for the past twenty-four hours
in your journal. As you sit quietly, consider your responsibility
for your involvement in and reaction to each situation. Note in your
journal some ideas of what you can do to address or remedy each
situation. Be as specific as possible. What will you do in the day ahead to
lighten the negativity in your life?

12   *The Core of the Matter*

It is easy to get lost in the maze of information, ideas, and advice about how to conduct a job search. In my mind, there are really only four basic issues to consider:

1.   *Your <u>purpose</u>.*
Your purpose is your reason for being here. For example, you may sense, on a fundamental level, that your reason for being on Earth is to help and encourage children.

2.   *Your <u>strengths</u>.*
Your strengths — what you are skilled at and enjoy — are the "pointers" to your purpose. For example, your strengths may be that you like to tell stories, you draw well, and you are a good writer.

3.   *Your <u>mission</u>.*
Your mission is what you choose to do to express your purpose. For example, you may decide that your mission is to create children's books.

4.   *Your <u>objective</u>.*
Your objectives are the specific actions you will take to get your mission done. For example, you may decide to seek out a job in a publishing house to get some hands-on training in producing books.

Today's Spiritual Guideline

Take some quiet time today to:

- Affirm that you have a purpose on this Earth.
- Petition for an open mind to the discoveries of the job-hunting journey.
- Give thanks for your strengths, whether they are clear to you at this time or not.

13 *Belonging*

Before we go further, I want to clear up one matter about this idea of "purpose." Yes, you have a specific purpose for which you have embarked on this search. But you also have a *generic* purpose: Each of us has the right to exist and be a part of creation.

I'll tell you a story. Several months ago, I was working with a man who had been fired from his job. The impact had been quite severe on him, as he was a very responsible, loving, caring husband and father, and the experience of having been put into this needy position was jarring. He loved his family deeply, and he was now uncertain about how he was going to continue to support them. His unemployment had brought him to a shaky and uncertain emotional state.

One afternoon when he came into my office for his regularly scheduled review of his job-search progress, I noticed that he looked particularly down and depressed. I asked him if he felt okay.

His response was, "Sometimes I feel like I don't belong."

We were both silent for a moment. Not certain of what I would say, I began to speak. "This morning as you came into the office, what did you see lining the sidewalks outside?" I asked.

"A row of beautiful spring flowers," he answered.

"Yes," I said. "I know they were planted by a gardener, but, when you look more deeply, who is responsible for their existence?"

"I believe God is," he said.

"And do you believe further that they belong there? Do they have a right and a purpose for existing along the sidewalk?"

"Of course," he said, and tears began to appear in his eyes. In that moment, he realized that he was at least as important as the flowers, that he belonged on the planet, doing exactly what he was doing.

Each of us has a generic purpose that, put simply, is to exist and be a part of all creation.

You belong here; you are entitled to, and freely given, your existence. Just as the flowers, trees, and animals belong and have a right to be precisely where they are, so do you. You are as essential and have the same right to exist as any other facet of creation.

Today's Spiritual Guideline

Consider this idea that you have a right to be where you are, that you belong. What feelings does this idea arouse in you?

Take some time today to write in your journal an affirmation to yourself that you belong here. As honestly as you can, record your feelings about this.

Think about any challenges this notion may present to your previously held beliefs. As specifically as possible, note these challenges in your journal.

14 *Chance*

Here's a thought: The odds against you arriving on this planet in the first place were astronomical.

Think about it. Millions of sperm cells had the opportunity to join with the egg cell that became you. Other egg cells had the opportunity to join with sperm cells, but did not prior to your formation. In biological terms, the odds against the specific formation that became you were literally millions to one.

And yet here you are.

The others who could have been formed are not here.

You are.

You were chosen from among millions of possible people.

Your appearance in this dimension at this time and in this place is no accident. It is the intention of creation and the Universe.

Meditate upon this truth.

Individual purpose is a thread in the tapestry. You are unique and special. You are essential to the beauty and completeness of the whole.

Today's Spiritual Guideline

As you sit quietly, review the events of yesterday (or today, if you are reading this in the evening). Sometime during the day, something happened that demonstrated your uniqueness. You did something that no one else could have done.

If some part of you is arguing that this is not true, I urge you to think again: Some action you did or thought or feeling you had was uniquely you.

Give yourself time to reflect on this. In your journal, record what you become aware of. Write a note of thanks for what makes you an individual like no other.

15 *My Grandfather*

As I write this, my ninety-five-year-old grandfather has just died. While preparing to travel to his funeral, my thoughts have been focused on his life. What, I wondered, was his purpose? As I meditated, repeating this question, this thought emerged:

He was one of the happiest, quietest, and most serene people I have ever encountered. He had both little and much in the way of material possessions at different points in his life. Still, his essential focus and approach to life remained the same: his faith, family, work, play. In quiet and peace. Always with a smile.

I think that was his purpose: To be content, no matter what life threw at him, no matter the current state of his physical and material prosperity.

His lesson is one we already know deep inside: Happiness is not a destination, it is the way.

The same is true of the job search process: Your search is part of the process, part of the way of your life. The fulfilling of your purpose is not so much in the job as it is in living every moment of every day of your life. It is in the moment-to-moment peace and tranquillity that comes as you are living out your purpose. That is the only way it can happen.

Today's Spiritual Guideline

Someone in your family or friendships has had an impact upon your life. You may have interpreted this impact either positively or negatively. Today, choose one person to write about in your journal. Consider that person's effect on your life and the lessons that the presence or actions of this person have taught you. Consider that this person, in addition to living out his or her own purpose, also helped illuminate your purpose. Reflect on this idea, and then note what you have learned, or are learning, from this person.

16 *Your Purpose Is Looking for You*

In addition to your generic purpose, you have a *specific* purpose, something you are sent here to do. This purpose is looking for you. It is seeking you out. It may hound you, invading your thoughts and depriving you of sleep. When you are out of your purpose, you may become nervous, irritable, dissatisfied all of the time. You may find your career an endless succession of job hops, each somewhat less satisfying than the one before. You may be wondering, *"What will it take to make me happy? How will I discover my purpose?"*

Today's Spiritual Guideline

I am going to ask something more of you today. I believe it is time, in your process, to set aside some dedicated time to doing an extended self-assessment. Yes, I know. I can hear you arguing that you have already done assessments, perhaps more than you'd like to remember. But I want to ask you to walk with me through a different kind of assessment, one with a spiritual dimension.

In fact, I believe these next steps are so critical to the process that I am going to ask you to make a commitment of time and space to do a special seven-step self-assessment. You may want to do one section each day for the next week. This is important. Take the time you need.

Will you make this choice for yourself? Write in your journal:

- a statement of commitment to this spiritual self-assessment
- a willingness to be open to whatever new learnings are in store for you
- a specific time plan for when you will do the seven assessment steps

17 What Paths Have You Been On?

The place to start is to become aware of any path that someone else has told you to follow. Advice or pressure or hidden expectations may have come from your peers, your classmates, parents, or a spouse. They may have, in good faith, intended to help you, but they may have led you to a path that is not yours.

Still, even a "wrong" path is a learning. The experience of following a path that did not work for you is firm and unequivocal guidance from the Universe that this is not your way. The real value is in the lessons that have been presented to you.

Reflect upon any unsatisfying experiences or jobs — either from your past or that you are now engaged in — that you felt compelled into by forces within or outside of yourself. Write in your journal about one of those experiences, describing it in detail, along with the reasons you now believe it was or is not the right path for you. This is not a time to blame others or dodge responsibility. Rather, this is a time to simply record the facts and your evaluation of what didn't work or isn't working.

From this vantage point, what are the lessons you can see? Record your observations. Be as specific as possible.

End this portion of the self-assessment by giving thanks for the variety of experiences and learnings you have had in your life.

18 *What Are Your Major Life Events?*

As you continue your self-assessment, keep in mind the Zen notion of always being a beginner on the path. This will help you to see with the wonder of a young child, to experience all as new.

Before you start this step of the assessment, gather some pens, pencils, and some blank paper. Arrange them to make your space as calming as possible. Then begin by slowing and clearing your mind. Take in a deep breath through your nose and exhale slowly through your mouth. While breathing slowly and deeply in this fashion, close your eyes for at least three minutes. During this brief meditative time, give silent thanks for the skills, abilities, and strengths you have been given. Dedicate this part of the assessment to your own personal benefit and the benefit of all you will serve in the course of your career. Slowly open your eyes and shift gradually out of your meditation.

For this portion of the assessment, I believe it is important that you write your responses by hand, rather than using a computer or word processor (unless, of course, there is a physical condition that necessitates a keyboard). Engaging in this direct contact and manual activity will help you consider your responses lovingly and carefully.

Start by considering the blank paper before you and give thanks for it. It will be a temporary container for your life's story. Label a page "LIFE EVENTS LIST."

Then, think back on the last ten years of your life. Jot down the major events that have occurred: jobs, projects, employment, personal issues, relationships, life changes. Write them without imposing judgment and without being concerned about technical details, such as chronological order.

To give you a clearer idea of how the steps of the assessment work together, I thought I'd offer some "real life" examples. For each of the assessment steps, I'll tell you about two people who consulted with me in their job search. Their assessments are abbreviated for the sake of this book, but I hope their process will give you some ideas and encouragement.

"Sue" came to me with a strong background in finance and accounting, and she had recently been laid off. "Bob" was an employed grade-school teacher, but he was feeling as if something was missing from his work and his life. Here's a sampling from their LIFE EVENTS LISTS:

Sue's Life Events List

I worked the counter at a fast-food restaurant.
I stocked shelves and worked as a cashier at the campus bookstore.
The local church paid me to keep their books.
I taught people on welfare the principles of personal financial management.
My first "real" job was auditing the financial records of nonprofit agencies for the state government.

Bob's Life Events List

I babysat a lot for my younger brothers and sisters.
I was a camp counselor during college summers.
I tutored elementary school children who were having reading problems.
I organized, wrote, and directed children's plays.
I coached college intramural and Little League baseball teams.
I was editor and writer for my college humor magazine.
I drew a giant mural for the neighborhood playground.
I told stories at the statewide storytelling festival.

After you have completed your LIFE EVENTS LIST, let it go for now and give yourself some time away from it. (If you do choose to continue on to Step Three later today, give yourself at least an hour of "breathing space" before you start again.)

19 *What Do You Do?*

SELF-ASSESSMENT STEP THREE

Look back over the LIFE EVENTS LIST you created in Step Two. Mark with a star or a check mark or highlighter pen those events, jobs, or projects that you particularly enjoyed or found significant in your life. Keep in mind that the only opinion that matters in this exercise is your own.

On a new piece of paper, summarize the special marked events, fleshing out the details as specifically as you can.

When you have finished, look back over your summaries for any "action verbs" that you can find. "Action verbs" describe what you actually did — such as built, repaired, wrote, developed, implemented, walked, ran, organized, drove, spoke, negotiated, addressed, taught, healed, listened, met, played, and so on. These verbs may be explicitly stated or implied within the context of your writing.

Make a thorough list of all these action verbs on a separate piece of paper. This is your ACTION LIST.

> ### Sue's Action List
> Worked the counter
> Took orders
> Filled orders
> Balanced the register
> Functioned as a cashier
> Stocked shelves
> Kept books
> Balanced checkbooks
> Reconciled accounts
> Taught
> Audited
> Helped people
> Monitored accounting standards

Bob's Action List

Babysat
Counseled
Taught
Organized
Wrote
Directed
Coached
Edited
Drew
Told stories
Played
Helped others create stories

Set your ACTION LIST aside for today; you will come back to it later. Now it is time to give yourself a break from the "action." Think of something refreshing and quieting that you could do for yourself at this moment. Go ahead . . . indulge in a little R&R. You deserve it.

20 *What Do You Enjoy?*

SELF-ASSESSMENT STEP FOUR

Return to your ACTION LIST. Think about how often you have performed these "actions" in your life. (Refer to your LIFE EVENTS LIST for guidance.) Now I want you to assign a "frequency number" to each action, assigning the highest number to the action you have performed the most and counting down to the action you have done the least. (Your highest number will vary, depending on how many actions you have on your list.)

Sue's Action List — with "frequency numbers" added

Worked the counter (2)
Took orders (4)
Filled orders (3)
Balanced the register (5)
Functioned as a cashier (6)
Stocked shelves (1)
Kept books (10)
Balanced checkbooks (7)
Reconciled accounts (8)
Taught (12)
Audited (13)
Helped people (11)
Monitored accounting standards (9)

Bob's Action List — with "frequency numbers" added

Babysat (1)
Counseled (3)
Taught (11)
Organized (9)
Wrote (8)
Directed (2)
Coached (7)
Edited (5)
Drew (10)
Told stories (12)
Played (4)
Helped others create stories (6)

On a new piece of paper, list your six top-ranked "actions," starting with the most frequent.

Sue's Frequent Action List	Bob's Frequent Action List
Audited	Told stories
Taught	Taught
Helped people	Drew
Kept books	Organized
Monitored accounting standards	Wrote
Reconciled accounts	Coached

Sit back for a few minutes to review your FREQUENT ACTION LIST. Think about how much you enjoyed (or didn't enjoy!) doing each of the actions listed.

Stick with me for one more list. This time I want you to take a sheet of paper and select the FREQUENT ACTIONS you like doing best. List them in the order you enjoy doing them and label this your ENJOYMENT LIST.

Sue's Enjoyment List	Bob's Enjoyment List
Helped people	Told stories
Taught	Wrote
Audited	Drew
Monitored accounting standards	Taught

Your FREQUENT ACTION LIST and your ENJOYMENT LIST may have items in the same or similar order. If so, good news! You truly enjoy all or much of what you are doing. If not, no problem! The point of the exercise is in the wisdom or the learning you discern. At times, the activities you perform most frequently may *not* be the ones you enjoy the most. This information can be just as helpful to you in revealing or illuminating the nature of your purpose.

21 | *What Are Your Strengths?*

SELF-ASSESSMENT STEP FIVE

We are coming to the core part of this assessment process. Set in front of you your FREQUENT ACTION LIST and your ENJOYMENT LIST. Study them carefully. What actions do you both *do* a lot and *enjoy*?

I want to ask you to make another list. (Just in case making lists is not your favorite activity, I urge you to keep on this path. Each time you make a new list, you are actually helping yourself see yourself from a new perspective!) Select three items that appear on <u>both</u> your FREQUENT ACTION LIST and your ENJOYMENT LIST that are the most appealing to you at this time.

List these actions that you perform frequently and enjoy performing on a new sheet of paper. Call it your DIRECTION LIST.

Sue's Direction List

Helped people
Taught
Audited

Bob's Direction List

Told stories
Drew
Wrote

Your DIRECTION LIST is very important because it shows your strengths. A strength is something you do well *and* enjoy doing. It is something that, when you are doing it, seems to cause you to pass outside of the realm of time. A strength flows. You have a sense of absorption, of personal satisfaction and fulfillment when you are doing it.

This is where you can begin to hone in on the heart of the matter. From your DIRECTION LIST, you can compile a STRENGTH LIST. (Take heart . . . this is the last list I'll ask you to make for a while!) For each item on your DIRECTION LIST, write a descriptive sentence for your STRENGTH LIST, using phrases such as:

I am good at . . .
I like to . . .
I enjoy . . .
I am skilled at . . .
I do _____ well . . .

Sue's Strength List

I like to help people.
I am skilled at teaching.
I understand principles and methods of auditing and their application.

Bob's Strength List

I enjoy telling stories.
I am good at drawing.
I am skilled at writing.

When you are satisfied with your STRENGTH LIST for now, find a reverent spot to store it. Then take a bit of time to reflect in silence. Give thanks for what has been and will be revealed to you.

When you have completed this part of the assessment, set your lists aside. If you have a window, open it, face it and breathe deeply. If possible, take a walk, offering silent appreciation for the world. If you are so inclined or have a need, eat, giving thanks for and savoring your food as you consume it. Give thanks for all. You are spiritually preparing yourself for the next step of this assessment. Your lists are extremely valuable. As you quietly consider their implications, they will begin to suggest to you the nature of your purpose.

22 What Is Your Current Understanding of Your Purpose?

SELF-ASSESSMENT STEP SIX

At this point, you are ready to make some notes for yourself about what your purpose might be.

Here's the key: Your specific purpose is revealed in your strengths. I believe your STRENGTH LIST is an expression of your purpose on this planet at this time. It is by no means the only expression of your purpose, and it may not be a complete description, but this list will strongly suggest where you should direct your attention as you approach the work of your life.

Today, create a calm place and time where you can feel at ease. Take your STRENGTH LIST and put it in a predominant place in front of you.

Look it over carefully, taking in what you do well and what you enjoy.

Keeping in mind that your sacred purpose is your reason for being here, let your STRENGTH LIST give you some ideas about your purpose. In looking at what you do well and enjoy, what do you sense is fundamental to your existence?

I want you to take what you know — and what you may only sense that you know — and write a statement of what you see as your purpose at this time. Your PURPOSE STATEMENT does not have to be "fancy." And it is not carved in stone! It is simply a summary of what you can see at this point in time about what you are called to do on this Earth.

Sue's Purpose Statement

Given my present understanding of myself and my strengths,
I sense that my sacred purpose, my reason for being on this Earth,
is to teach money management to people in need.

Bob's Purpose Statement

With what I know about myself and my life at this time,
I believe that my sacred purpose, my reason for being on this Earth,
is to help and encourage children understand themselves
and their world through pictures and stories.

Set your PURPOSE STATEMENT aside for now; you will come back to it later.

End your time today by giving silent thanks for all the talents, gifts, and experiences you have been given. Give thanks for the people who are a part of both your personal and professional life. Give thanks for the journey you are on.

23 How Are You Living, or Not Living, Your Purpose?

SELF-ASSESSMENT STEP SEVEN

Once you have begun to identify your purpose, you will be immediately faced with more uncertainty. If, for example, you sense your purpose in life is to educate and inform, then you will need to decide how you might put your purpose into action.

Pull out a recent résumé you have prepared. (Or, if you don't have a résumé, simply write a list of jobs you have had, briefly describing the kind of work you have done in each.)

Compare your past jobs and work that you have done in your past employment to your PURPOSE STATEMENT.

Ask yourself this question: *"Have I served my purpose, expressed my purpose, at least in part, in any of these jobs?"*

If so, in your journal, record as many ways as you can find in which your purpose has been expressed, based on your current understanding of that purpose.

If you have found no purposeful moments in any of your employment experiences, then it's time for some soul-searching. Clearly, your purpose and your livelihood have somehow become separated. You may be experiencing physical ailments. Your body may be giving you signals that you are living an essentially dis-integrated life. This is the time to take some re-directive and re-integrative steps. Your purpose is still there, whether it has been expressed in your work life up to now or not. Start by writing down as many specific ways as you can in which you have been deflected away from your purpose.

24 *Expressing Purpose*

If you say that something is vital
and central to your life,
and yet you don't do it
every day of your life,
then it is not vital and central.

Like prayer.
Like meditation.
Like writing.
Like expressing your life's purpose through a certain vocation.

Today's Spiritual Guideline

Ponder these questions:

- What is vital to me today?
- This month?
- This year?
- In my lifetime?

Jot down in your journal what comes to mind.

Then ask yourself:

- Am I acting on what I believe to be vital?

Note in your journal one thing you could do in the day ahead that would contribute to what is central to your life.

25 *Ease Up*

If you've come this far in the book, you've done a lot of good work. You've taken vital steps toward understanding your purpose. The time has come to ease up on yourself.

This, too, is a crucial step along the path toward finding purpose, but many people miss it.

Most searches involves a lot of thinking, planning, and doing, just like you have been engaged in during this process of assessment.

Now I am going to ask you to stop doing anything for a moment.

When we are in constant motion, whether internally or externally, we miss a lot of what is going on around us. And when we don't take time to really notice, our thoughts may impose a quick interpretation about what is happening and may distort the truth. We miss what really is.

What would it be like, for this day, simply to observe what is taking place? To suspend all judgments, all thoughts such as, "That would be the best job for me," or "I'd never like to do that," or "I have been treated unfairly," or other similar interpretations that you might habitually place upon events?

When you suspend judgment, you may be amazed at what else you notice. Giving yourself some "time off" from making conclusions will give your sense of purpose a chance to clarify and take shape — for it is there, ever before you. You may even wonder why you weren't able to see it before!

Give it a try. For one day, simply observe, accept, and give silent, inner thanks for the opportunity to be a part of creation. Give thanks for the gift of life this day, regardless of what is happening.

Today's Spiritual Guideline

As you move through the day ahead, simply and quietly observe what is happening. Do not try to place any specific interpretations on what you experience.

Allow your senses to be engaged. Observe other people, the weather, birds and other animals, plant life. Notice the smells. Feel the air around you. Listen to what others have to say — really listen. Do not attempt to impose your own opinion; only offer acceptance of what is. Listen and observe.

At the end of the day, take time to record what you noticed. Don't try to read meaning into the day. Simply record your observations in your journal and give thanks for your life this day.

26 *Dream Lessons*

While you are developing a spiritual practice and applying it to this journey, you have available many channels of learning. An often overlooked source of inner messages and lessons is our dreams. Expressions of our purpose can be presented during these nightly episodes.

Many years ago I studied to become a Roman Catholic priest, although I decided not to continue those studies. In a recent dream I found myself in the sacristy of the parish in which I grew up, a room in which I had spent a great deal of time as an altar boy. The sacristy was crowded with priests and altar boys preparing for a major ceremony. I realized that I was to be a participant in the ceremony and that I would need to find some vestments to wear.

At this point it occurred to me that they might be running out of vestments, so I hurried back to the closet where I knew they kept cassocks and surplices for the altar boys. I found that all the traditional black cassocks, those worn by parish priests, were gone. However, there remained another kind of robe not immediately familiar to me. I grabbed it and hurried back to the priests' vesting area. When I put the robe on and looked into the mirror, to my surprise I was wearing the brown hooded robe of a Franciscan monk.

As I thought about this dream, it occurred to me that perhaps my role as a career counselor is more like a monk's than a priest's, more brother than father. Perhaps I have been called to be the one who encourages, coaches, and suggests rather than the one who leads and directs. Perhaps I am called to live as part of a community rather than as one who stands alone in a place of special leadership.

The dream helped me see that I have a different kind of ministry in the world, with its own spiritual purpose, than I would have had as a priest. In linking the notion of spirituality with career and the living out of my purpose, I believe I am fulfilling my role as a "monk. "

Your dreams can reveal such messages to you. Practice observing carefully and without judgment the events of your dreams. They are an important and rich source of guidance and love, and they are available to you now.

Today's Spiritual Guideline

Before you go to sleep tonight, promise yourself that you will remember at least one of tonight's dreams. It might be helpful to keep your journal beside your bed so you can record the dream immediately upon waking.

Read slowly and carefully through the events of your dream and spend some time reflecting on your dream. What is there in this dream that speaks to your current journey? It might relate to your mission, objective, methods, or direction. It might suggest contacts or new possibilities.

In your journal, make note of any insights your dream has given you and any specific actions the dream might suggest to you.

27 Dream Possibilities

Allow yourself to dream a little,
    for what we call "real"
    had its beginnings in nothingness.

From General Motors to Microsoft,
    from a kitten to a human child,
    from a flower to a large green zucchini,
it all started from what appeared to be nothing.

So today give your dreams free rein,
    knowing that the difference between them
    and what is considered "real"
is only in your imagination.

Today's Spiritual Guideline

Continue to open yourself to the assistance of your dreams
on this journey. Simply be attentive to the content of your
dreams tonight. Do nothing more.

28 *Silence*

As I organize my thoughts to fulfill this day's purpose,
I will consult the silence within.
I will suspend judgment.
I will allow myself to be the creation
    that belongs
    that glorifies its Creator
    that permits and encourages all of creation to belong
    and glorify its Creator.
And so I go silent and listen.

Today's Spiritual Guideline

As a part of your spiritual discipline in the day ahead, practice some moments of silence. For a space of at least ten minutes, look for nothing more than silence to fill your time. Simply be still and quiet. Try this three times during this day. If possible, extend your period of silence up to an hour.

At the end of the day, write in your journal what those experiences were like for you. What did you notice? How did you feel? What differences did periods of silence make in your day? In your outlook? In your emotional life? In your physical life?

29 *Living with Ambiguity*

We can be certain of one fact: Life will never go the way we think it should go. We cannot predict the future with any accuracy. And this frustrates us. Most of us find ambiguity very difficult to live with.

Yet if everything were predictable, we would not have to expend any physical, mental or spiritual energy on the issue at hand. We would not have to think. We would not have to meditate or pray. We would not have to exert any extra energy. We could just vegetate. And while this may be the easier path, it ultimately ends in boredom, restlessness, and dissatisfaction.

The other path, the path of work, prayer — even play — is a much more exciting and enriching path. There are unlimited opportunities for learning and fun, and chances to profit, both materially and spiritually.

The deeply spiritual path requires a commitment both to spiritual and physical action. Yet there is a paradox. If we strive too hard for something, we may lose it. One of the secrets is to be willing to wait, to be open in meditative silence for what comes to us. There is no certainty in this waiting. You cannot predict what will happen. But you can be certain that you have the capacity to respond and act in harmony with the Universe.

Today's Spiritual Guideline

In your journal, write about something that happened in the last twenty-four hours that you didn't expect or couldn't have predicted. Based on your initial reaction to it, how did this event either contribute to or hinder your progress on the job-search journey?

Put your journal aside and go into silence for a time, preferably at least fifteen minutes. Now go back to what you wrote and think again.

Ask yourself these questions:

- How did this event impact my journey?
- What are the lessons that are offered here?
- How will I respond?

Note in your journal what comes to mind this time.

30 *Chaos*

I give thanks for the chaos in my life.
It is the stuff of creativity.

If I understood everything,
      if everything made perfect sense all the time
      if everything conformed to my notions
      of what ought to be
there would be no room for growth.

Chaos forces me to learn,
      to grow
      to organize
      to respond creatively.

I watch a small child
      responding to and learning from
      what must, to her,
      seem like total chaos all the time.

It doesn't even slow her down!
      She'll impose her own order and meaning,
      even if we don't like it
      or disagree.
And she will soar as a result.

I give thanks for chaos,
      for all the stuff that doesn't make sense
      for all the chances for something new to happen.
It is the stuff of creativity.

Today's Spiritual Guideline

Note something that happened in the past twenty-four hours that didn't appear to make sense. Spend time in silence, reflecting on this event.

It is possible that this event will never make sense. Perhaps the lesson is that it is not necessary for you to understand everything. Or perhaps what appears as chaos is calling for a new response from you, a new way of looking at things.

For today, simply record in your journal your response to the apparent chaos and end with a petition to be open to what else the chaos might have to bring you.

3 | *Answers*

Sometimes we want to have the answer NOW.
The whole answer — complete and unambiguous.

But that is not the way the Universe works.
It is both complete and incomplete.
It is both ambiguous and unambiguous.

We know what we need to do,
and yet we don't know.

Answers come,
and yet they are insubstantial;
they melt like the snow.

The answers will come.
Then they will change.

Today's Spiritual Guideline

Job-search experiences are fundamentally ambiguous.
Surety appears to be a rare thing. The helpful question is,
"How much ambiguity can I live with?" Take some time to reflect on this
question in your journal.

If you find that your tolerance for ambiguity is being stretched, consider
some practical ways in which you can reduce ambiguity in areas of your
life that don't involve the job search. What things can you count on? What
things are within your control? List them in your journal.

Claiming the reassurances that you do have in your life will help you
extend your tolerance for the unknown.

32 *Paradox I*

A spiritual friend of mine once said,
"The opposite of everything is always true."

That statement was both correct and incorrect at the same time.
It is the eternal paradox of life and death
    of good and bad
    of love and fear
    of happiness and sadness.
They are two sides or aspects of the same thing.

Here I am between employment and unemployment,
between ideal employment and gross mismatch.
My job search is unfinished,
and yet every action I take is complete.

Today's Spiritual Guideline

Imagine this for a moment: What if you were doing the exact opposite of what you are doing now? How might your life be different? How might you feel? Are there lessons for you in considering the opposite path? What might they be? Write the ideas that occur to you in your journal.

33 _Meeting Your Mission_

By now, you have assessed yourself in a multitude of ways. You have gone within to consult sacred wisdom. You may have also taken assessment tests with a career consultant, psychologist, or other professional. You may have consulted friends and co-workers. Perhaps you have begun to sense a larger pattern to your strengths, a potential purpose for your existence.

There is another layer to consider. It is time once again to go deep within, to exercise your spiritual practice, to consider what your mission in life might be. Your mission is what you choose to do to _express_ your purpose.

Go back for a moment to the two people whose examples you've been following. Sue, who felt her purpose was to teach money management to those in need, began to envision that her mission might be to manage funds for a charitable organization.

Bob, whose purpose appeared to be helping children understand themselves and their world though stories and pictures, began to see that his mission might be to create children's books.

Whatever your mission is, if you are going to present it to potential employers, business partners, friends — anyone — you will need some concrete words to convey your thoughts.

If the thought of stating how you might accomplish your life's purpose is daunting, know this: As a part of your spiritual practice, you are constantly flowing and fulfilling your purpose. No "mission statement" can ever completely contain your reality. The statement you make today is simply an acknowledgment of what you know at the moment.

Today's Spiritual Guideline

Before you begin today, I urge you to clear enough time for this exercise so you won't have outside pressure to "hurry." Start by spending some meditative time reviewing your self-assessment lists. Consider what you have learned. Set these materials aside for now.

If you have a special place in your life for meditation and prayer, go there. Enter into deep silence. Spend as long as you need in this state. Ask yourself again: *"What do I understand at this time to be my sacred purpose in life?"*

Don't worry if a sense of certainty eludes you. Accept in love and trust that your uncertainty is a friend and teacher. For now, trusting whatever inner understanding you have of your purpose, let yourself consider how you might put that purpose into action. In your journal, jot down the ideas that occur to you.

Take some time to reflect on these ideas. Then select one that attracts you at this particular time. Don't worry about picking the "right" one. Any choice you make at this point flows directly from the work you have already done to explore and understand your sacred purpose.

Write a simple sentence describing one way in which you can envision putting your purpose into action. For example,

Sue's Mission
Since I want to teach money management to those in need,
I can envision assisting charitable organizations
with accounting and money management.

Bob's Mission
Since I want to help children understand themselves
through stories and pictures,
I can envision creating children's books.

Don't get bogged down in making a formal "mission statement." Do not be concerned about the correctness or incorrectness of your format. Simply state what comes to you and acknowledge that it is sacred wisdom.

34 *Paradox II*

"That job sounds like it would be good for me. But I'm also considering this other. Which one best expresses my purpose?"

This may be what you experience during your job search. Contradictory and paradoxical information. How do you know when something is "right"?

These are difficult and challenging questions. They strike at the core of job search. They strike at the core of spirituality. They strike at the very heart of life.

This is precisely why there can be no formulaic answers to this quest — or any other quest. The spiritual approach permits the emergence of more than one way to express your purpose! And some of those missions may be paradoxical indeed. Yet, if you approach your search from your spiritual core, any mission that contributes directly to the fulfillment of your ultimate purpose on Earth is valuable. There is no "right" or "wrong" mission.

Whenever you choose to respond to life in purpose-affirming ways, you are traveling the path you need to be on. In the course of your job search, if your response affirms your determination to hold to what you have come to understand as your purpose, you will make the best decision for you.

Remain faithful to your spiritual practice, listen to the wisdom and lessons that are revealed, and you will be guided. Integrate this practice with all your job-search actions, and you will do it the "right" way. There is no other way you can do it.

Relax. Deep within, you know that you are guided, that wisdom is available.

Today's Spiritual Guideline

This is a good time to check in with yourself to see how your commitment to a daily spiritual practice is coming along. If you find that you have wandered from your original intention to a specific, three-times-a-day spiritual practice, go back to page 18 and re-read the commitment statement you wrote in your journal. Make any changes to it that you need to in order to fit with your lifestyle. It is better to make a commitment that you can honor than to add to your guilt or frustration by making a commitment that is nearly impossible to keep.

Write in your journal a renewed commitment to a spiritual practice as the foundation for your journey.

Think back over the spiritual practices and exercises that you have completed so far. What have you perceived that you want to act on in the day ahead to move yourself forward? Note in your journal what comes to mind.

35 When the Paradoxes of Life Come to Visit

When the paradoxes of life come to visit you, welcome them in. It surely means that you are on the verge of a new, unique, and exciting turn in your life.

If you are wondering what I mean by this, perhaps this story will help.

A client entered my office one afternoon with a puzzled look on his face. He was quite accomplished in computer programming, as well as systems design and construction, and in recent years he had also acquired some experience in human resources training and recruiting. He was now pursuing the mission of combining his interests in human resources and information systems, but he was not yet sure how this could be done. To assist him in his quest, he had been meeting with and interviewing acknowledged authorities in both fields. But now he was confused.

One source, an information systems expert, had assured him that, beyond a shadow of doubt, he must concentrate his energies primarily in the field of computers and information management. If he did that, there was no way he could go wrong.

Another source, an extremely successful human resources consultant, instructed him to concentrate his efforts on the people management side. Human resources, she explained, is widely acknowledged to be the hottest field going as we enter the next century.

What should he believe? Here were two highly credible sources sending him in apparently different directions.

Both sources had a view of the truth. Both gave my client valuable information. Now, the question for him was what to do with this information in light of what he knew his purpose to be.

After consulting his inner wisdom, he saw that it was not an "either/or" decision. He saw that, as a result of his unique training, experience, and personal inclinations, he could combine information management technologies with the softer art of human resources management. He decided to become a human resources information specialist. This meant he could bring state-of-the-art computers into the human resources department and demonstrate how these devices could help do the essential tasks better. By combining two apparent opposites, he was cutting a path to something new and innovative. He was suddenly excited and enthusiastic about the new direction suggested by these paradoxical encounters.

Today's Spiritual Guideline

While on this journey, you have probably already received or gathered advice from many sources — books, tapes, family, friends, professionals. Some of it may be contradictory. The central question is, "What do *you* think about it?"

In your journal, note what advice seems helpful or contributory to your sense of mission and purpose. Note what advice seems contradictory. Step back a moment and take a deeper look. Is there anything in this "contradictory" advice that suggests a new possibility? Journal about what advice seems useful to pay attention to at this time.

36 *The Objective*

The decisions never seem to end, do they? Well, the paradox is, neither do the possibilities.

Once you have an idea in your mind of a possible mission, you'll need to think about how you could accomplish this mission. What steps, training, learning, changing will you need to put your mission into action? These details, what you will do to accomplish your mission, comprise what I call an objective. Think of an objective as a practical tool that will help potential employers understand what it is you want to do.

We are often told that there is a right way, or a better way, to get things done. Well, that all depends upon what you are trying to accomplish.

Consider Sue's mission for a moment: To assist nonprofit agencies with accounting and money management. When she began to think of how she could accomplish that mission, here are some objectives she thought of:

Sue's Possible Objectives

Find a job as an accountant with a social service agency.

Work for a bank that assists charitable organizations.

Act as a consultant to one or more nonprofit agencies.

Serve as a board member of such an agency.

Teach or train other professional or paraprofessional persons in sound accounting principles for the nonprofit sector.

Bob's mission, on the other hand, was to create children's books. His list of objectives looked like this:

Bob's Possible Objectives

Find an entry-level job at a publisher specializing in children's books.

Study and learn creative writing techniques. [*Occasionally, education may be an integral part of the objective.*]

Apprentice to an illustrator of children's books.

Sell children's books as a way of learning more about what's available.

Work at a design or print shop.

The way is "right" if it gets you where you want to go.

Today's Spiritual Guideline

So far in this process, you have created three lists or statements that I believe are key to your search: a list of your STRENGTHS, a statement of your PURPOSE as you understand it at this time, and a possible MISSION that expresses your purpose.

Gather these three papers in front of you today. If you would like, copy these three items into your journal, updating them with any new information you have discovered about yourself.

Take a step back for a moment to gain additional perspective. Let the accuracy of what you have written sink in.

Then give yourself some quiet time to consider some specific ways you might put your mission into action. Don't make judgments about what is the "best" way. Simply write down any POSSIBLE OBJECTIVES that occur to you that might help you accomplish your mission.

37 *Focusing on Your Objective*

The spiritual life, because of its focus on being "open," might seem to mitigate the setting of precise objectives. A profound reliance on sacred, spiritual wisdom might appear to make such definitive pronouncements unnecessary.

In truth, at the core of our spiritual being — and certainly as we continue the job search — taking action is a necessary part of life. Another paradox!

By setting an objective, you are expressing, in greater detail, what you think you need to do in order to accomplish your mission.

Today's Spiritual Guideline

Look at the list of POSSIBLE OBJECTIVES that you have created. Spend some time considering them.

Select one that seems to fit for you at this time. Don't worry about picking the "right" one. Rather, choose one that honestly feels that it could serve as a physical expression of what you understand your mission to be. Write it in your journal on a separate page. Be specific.

This is an excellent time to make use of friends or family members to determine if your objective is clear. Does it state what you want to do? Does it accomplish your mission?

I encourage you not to be discouraged if, the first time, the objective you have written does not clearly communicate your sense of mission to others. You may find that you want to refine your objective many times, write it again, try out several different objectives. The important matter is to continually hold your sense of purpose and mission before you. An objective simply serves to keep you on the path to that purpose.

38 *Rest*

In the midst of any job search — even a spiritual job search! — it is entirely possible to become obsessed with finding the right job, with making all the right moves and choices, with doing the right things, with having everything in the search be right, right, right. At times, you may even think that your spiritual practice is not right, or that you have not been approaching it in the right way or with the proper discipline.

It is very important to permit yourself some rest, to let up on the pressure you may have put on yourself. Rest is as much a spiritual practice as work — perhaps even more so, although our culture would not have us believe that.

When you rest, your body and spirit are renewed. You will then be prepared to re-enter the search with vigor and with joy.

Today's Spiritual Guideline

Take a break. Give yourself a day or a weekend off.

Yes, I can hear the arguments. And, yes, I know how much you need it. Here is what I say to you: You are responsible for making a choice to rest. And it is an important choice.

During your "time off," remove all thoughts about your job search from your conscious mind. Engage in purely recreational activities, or do nothing. For your spiritual practice, enter into periods of quiet meditation only. Offer prayers of thanksgiving, but no petitions or questions. Allow the quiet and peace to simply *BE*. Remove the frenzy from both your physical and spiritual world. The rest and refreshment that you need will be given to you.

39 The Résumé Ritual

As I peruse the classified ads and yellow pages, I find an abundance of advertising for résumé services. Books abound on the subject as well. And I have been personally present at innumerable discussions and debates on the best way to write and present a résumé. "Do it the right way," the reasoning often goes, "and the recipients won't be able to resist granting you an interview, possibly even a job."

And yet résumés don't get jobs — people do. The résumé will, in fact, be of little value unless it is targeted to the specific and timely needs of a potential employer. Uncounted beautiful and well thought-out résumés quickly find their way into the trash when sent unsolicited to an employer who has no need for the apparent skills of the sender.

Still, our preoccupation with the résumé suggests that it has a deeper meaning than just a job-finding tool. In a very real way, it represents our vocational and personal identity, something deep and spiritual about who we are. While the résumé is not the only piece in the job-finding puzzle by any means, we know, almost instinctively, that this exercise is important.

On one level, the document you produce is your "sales brochure," the tool you will use to get the potential employer's attention and make him or her remember you. On a deeper, and perhaps more important level, the résumé-writing process serves other purposes:

- creating affirmations about yourself
- taking inventory of your skills
- documenting your expertise
- taking note of your accomplishments
- naming your ability to handle certain tasks
- identifying the direction you want to be headed in
- creating an overall statement of your mission and, at least by implication, your purpose on Earth

Today's Spiritual Guideline

If you have already written a résumé, re-read it today, noting in your journal what message it conveys about your purpose, your mission (how you will express your purpose), and your objective (what you will do to accomplish your mission). Is there anything about your résumé that doesn't "ring true" with the spiritual self-assessments you have been doing? Compare your résumé with your objective statement. Does it support what you want to do to fulfill your mission? How? If it doesn't, consider how you might accurately and honestly communicate your experience, tailoring it to support your current objective. Make some notes to yourself in your journal about what you might like to change.

If you are just starting the résumé ritual, I recommend some of the excellent books available to help guide you. In the Bibliography at the back of this book, I have listed several books that offer résumé assistance. Today would be a good day to select one to help you get started. Whatever process you decide to use, keep your statements of purpose, mission, and objective clearly displayed in front of you to help you stay focused on where you are headed.

Above all, I urge you to trust the inner work you have been doing and what you have discovered about yourself.

40 *Openness*

Today I will cultivate a sense of
openness to everything that happens.
Everything.

I will trust that it all fits together
in ways I can't even imagine.

The surprises are there
under my nose,
waiting to be discovered,
yearning to reveal themselves
if I will but pay attention.

Just as in each breath I take in,
the molecules find their form and pattern,
and, without my even asking, make me live,
so too, I need not consciously ask for meaning.

Purpose and fulfillment are freely offered to me,
in this moment, and the next, and the next.

Today's Spiritual Guideline

Think back on the events of the preceding day. What was
freely offered to you without your even asking? List these
gifts in your journal and give thanks for them. Then note as specifically as
you can how these gifts have assisted you on your job quest.

41 | *Résumé Preparation*

As I prepare to work on my résumé,
my purpose is ever before me.

I want to
    reflect
    express
    spotlight
how I see living out my purpose.

Let my résumé communicate
    who I am
    where I am headed.
Let it be a fair and accurate report of
    what I know
    what I have accomplished
    what I want to do.
Let it be a vehicle to bring these
    to the attention of those I need.

I recognize this as a sacred task.
I will honor my inner understanding
as I consider my choices.

Today's Spiritual Guideline

Spend some extra time today in a quiet place. Do some slow, deep breathing. As you feel your breath move in and out of your body, allow yourself to feel a sense of opening to what is ahead. If fears or concerns enter your mind, breathe through them with another deep, satisfying breath.

Your only spiritual task for today is to rest in the knowledge that there is a reason why you are here, that your purpose is finding you.

42 *Surfacing*

As you prepare or revise your résumé, you will be coming face-to-face with your past. In that process, you may find some aspects of your life coming to the surface that need healing, perhaps some unpleasant actions, reactions, or experiences. Or perhaps you may notice something about your personality that has been preventing you from fully entering the rich flow of your life. Or perhaps there are people in your life who have acted as filters or dams, holding you back, keeping you from learning and fulfilling your purpose.

Sometimes strong feelings begin to surface. Anger, unexpected and sometimes seemingly overwhelming, is often reported among job and career seekers. Forms of depression, which are often related, may also appear.

Listen carefully: This is normal and natural, and something that many of us experience. If you resist the surfacing of these feelings and reactions, they may come back at a later time, possibly stronger than before. You may want to enlist the help of an objective professional to help you understand your feelings. This might be the time to approach someone from your past to ask for, or give, forgiveness. You may need to forgive yourself.

Whatever you do, do not fight your feelings. Integrate them into your spiritual practice. When you are feeling angry, for example, and you find yourself speaking or behaving in uncharacteristic or unpredictable ways, it is a signal to pause. Go to a quiet place where you can experience the feeling without hurting yourself or others. Find safe outlets for your anger, in physical activity, for example. Give thanks for the ability to cleanse and integrate your feelings. Then offer petitions that you may be granted the wisdom to see the learnings and opportunities for growth even in negative experiences.

Remember that the spiritual process is both an awakening process and a self-correcting process. We awaken to new opportunities, and we discover areas where we are in need of growth, development, or correction.

Today's Spiritual Guideline

Give yourself some quiet time to reflect on any feelings from your past that are surfacing for you. Make note of them in your journal, without judging whether they are "good" or "bad." Recognize them for what they are — your feelings — without attaching value.

Record in your journal a prior time in your life when anger or other strong emotions have risen to the surface. As you look back on that time, what learnings came out of that experience?

Consider your current feelings:

- What can I learn from how I feel today?
- Is there anyone I need to talk with about how I feel? To ask forgiveness, or to forgive?
- Is there anything I need to do for myself, so I can accept my feelings and move on?

Write in your journal any specific actions you will take and when you will do them.

43 *Personal History*

Throughout time, many spiritual masters have taught us that what has gone before in our lives does not necessarily directly determine what will happen now or in the future. For example, Jesus spent his early years training to be a carpenter, yet, as far as we know, he never practiced the trade during his adult life. Clearly, his purpose was quite different from his training.

This is a remarkably difficult concept for us to grasp. Almost everything we've been taught to hold sacred, when it comes to career life, seems to run counter to this idea. "You must have a history, you must have a track record and you must do only what your past has expressly prepared you to do," is the litany we most often are told.

You have learned much through your personal history, but that history does not define you, that history is not you, nor does it dictate what you can become. Yet, in the composition of a résumé, you are forced to use your history to support a present-moment career objective.

You may be spending too much time in regret or analysis or paralysis, or you may be suffering the effects of some past decision. Here's a secret: It is the learnings that you have acquired throughout your past that are important.

The time of the résumé is paradoxical. It is the perfect opportunity to consider your history and learn from it. It is also the perfect opportunity to heal your personal history and set a new direction in peace and confidence.

Today's Spiritual Guideline

Find a red pen (or some other vivid color) and write in your journal about what you would honestly like removed from your past. Draw a red circle around what you have written to symbolize that your past is in the past.

Here are some thoughts to consider:

- My past will always be a part of me, but it does not have to rule me.
- I own my past; it does not own me.
- My past does not solely determine my future.
- No matter what my past is, I have unlimited opportunities to learn from it.

Take some quiet time to reflect on the hold your past has on you and what you may need freedom from — especially in your heart or in your head. Then, using a different color pen, note your thoughts in your journal.

44 _Is This Résumé Done?_

One common problem with résumés is trying to force your entire personal history into a kind of artificially constructed whole. I have on occasion received résumés that were in excess of ten pages long! The authors were presenting everything they had ever done and assuming that I, as a human resources professional, would make some sense or direction out of it. Do not let someone else impose direction on your career. That is your responsibility. The rubric of the résumé gives you the opportunity to publicly state your current objective.

From a spiritual perspective, there is only one question for you to ponder as you complete your résumé: _"Does this résumé support and communicate the living out of my mission, fulfilling my life's purpose?"_

Consider and honestly apply this question to each portion of your résumé as you work with it.

Today's Spiritual Guideline

Give yourself some time to consider this fundamental question: _"Does my résumé communicate the living out of my mission?"_ If your mission is muddled or unclear in your résumé, make some changes.

Ask friends and trusted associates to review your résumé. Ask them what they see in it, what it communicates to them. If it does not communicate what you sense your true mission to be, make some more changes.

Only when it communicates the message of your mission, to your personal satisfaction, are you finished. That doesn't mean you have to finish it all today! It means that only you can decide when it is complete. Pause in silence to give thanks for this wonderful, helpful document.

45 *Lighten Up*

A friend gave me some excellent advice today:

"You're taking this way too seriously.
Lighten up. Enjoy your life."

Of course, she was right.

I am too serious
>about my career
>about my own importance
>about deadlines
>about the expectations of others
>about the weather
>about money
>about life.

Life is important, but it is not always serious.
Only we are.

Today's Spiritual Guideline

Make a plan to do something "just for fun" in the next twenty-four hours. If that seems like a difficult task to manage on your own, find someone to help you lighten up. Give your body and mind a chance to experience the not-so-serious side of life.

46 Getting Started Each Day

You may start each day not knowing what you are going to do that day. That is perfectly acceptable. In fact, actively approaching the day with an attitude of openness and flow is preferable to a high degree of structure.

This is not to say that you should not plan. In fact, quite the opposite. It is fitting that you quietly and meditatively consider where you need to go, how you need to proceed each day. It is appropriate to commit these plans to writing and to record your activities in a systematic way. This is part of the order and flow of your daily process.

The problems that we create for ourselves begin when we become attached to the plan. A plan is a doorway, a beginning step on the path. But all plans are subject to revision. If we fool ourselves into believing that ours is the "master plan," then not only do we become obsessed and unhappy, but we also close ourselves off to the full range of human experience that is available to us each day.

This is another paradox for your consideration: *"I know what I am going to do today. I don't know what I am going to do today."* Both can be true!

In order to begin each day, you do need a plan. And yet, as you develop and implement that plan, you need a sense of openness and flexibility as you enter the flow of the day. The key is having the freedom to respond to what is given you.

Today's Spiritual Guideline

As an experiment, set aside one day of your search with no agenda. Do not generate a schedule or plan of any kind. Let the day flow naturally. This doesn't mean do nothing. Quite the contrary. Go out and do what seems appropriate. Do what you need and want to do to move forward on the journey.

At the end of this day, carefully record in your journal what happened.

Consider what you need for balance:

- If you found the spontaneous unfolding of this day helpful, how you might be more open to flexibility on future days?

- If this day was unproductive for you, how might you might want to take more care in planning and focusing on future days?

Write your thoughts in your journal.

47 Vesting

Everything we do is part of the sacred. Every ordinary act, even something as simple as getting dressed in the morning, can be a spiritual practice.

In my younger days, when I was an altar boy in the local Catholic church, we used to observe the priest as he put on his vestments prior to mass. This process of vesting included certain rituals and silent prayers as the priest dressed in each article of sacramental clothing. Although I did not understand it at the time, I found this quiet, private ceremony to be beautiful and meaningful in its simplicity.

Rituals can help us get in touch with the sacred. Rituals can set certain tasks and activities apart, and help us acknowledge and affirm their sacred status.

Imagine this: Each day as you prepare to meet the task of seeking your mission and purpose, you add a ritual to your routine acts of preparation to help prepare you spiritually. For example, your ritual could be something as simple as a brief pause before your morning washing or a moment of silence as you begin to dress.

Whatever fits for you, I urge you to give it a try. A simple morning ritual will remind you that what you seek is not only a job or career; it is a sacred purpose that is directly connected to your reason for being.

Today's Spiritual Guideline

As a part of your spiritual practice for the day ahead, introduce a small ritual in the morning as you dress: Select a "vestment" to wear for the day — perhaps a special scarf, or tie, or pin. Something that will remind you that this journey you are on is sacred and central to your life.

At the end of the day, record in your journal what effect wearing your "vestment" had on you.

Consider and decide what morning rituals you will continue or add to the next day.

48 _Commuter Meditation_

As you are preparing to leave for whatever appointments, research, meetings, or work you have planned for the day, you can enhance your connection with the spiritual by practicing a simple "commuter meditation." Making a regular practice of this will introduce a sense of peace into your day.

If you will be driving, gather your things for the day and get into your car. Insert the key, fasten the seat belt, lock the doors, and do whatever else you need to get comfortable and settled. Relax and become still in your seat.

If you will be commuting by bus or train, take a moment to sit in a comfortable chair in your house just before you leave. Have all of your things for the day gathered so you can be settled. Relax and become still in your chair.

- Close your eyes.
- Breathe slowly and deeply. With each inhalation, say quietly to yourself: _"Thank you for this day."_
- With each exhalation, say: _"Guide me into the flow of purpose."_
- Repeat this at least three times, more if you desire.
- Go into silence for about a minute, concentrating only on the sound of your breathing.
- Slowly open your eyes.
- Finish with a deep breath.

Practicing this meditation every day will only take a few minutes, and it will immensely foster your awareness of your purpose.

Today's Spiritual Guideline

Just before you practice the commuter meditation this morning (or tomorrow morning, if you are reading this in the evening), take time to describe in your journal how you are feeling about the day ahead of you.

Then try the meditation.

Instead of leaving immediately after you have finished the meditation, take another few minutes to note in your journal any thoughts or feelings that may have changed for you during the meditation, or anything that you are aware of after the meditation that you hadn't noticed before.

49 *Coincidence*

In the flow of the spiritually-based job search, there is no such thing as coincidence. The question is whether or not we will see and receive the lesson or let it pass us by.

Five years ago my one-year-old son, Will, died suddenly and without warning. A few years after, on the date of his birthday, I arrived at my office as usual, yet my mood was anything but upbeat. Throughout the day, my thoughts were with my son and the glorious birthday celebration we could have had if only he were here. I fought back tears repeatedly, but I didn't say anything to my co-workers; I considered my mourning a private matter.

The day wore on, and by mid-afternoon I felt that I might make it through the day. Suddenly, our chief engineer, Ronnie, appeared at my office door. He was smiling; beaming would have been an even better description.

"Well, Bill," he said, "aren't you going to have some birthday cake?"

"What?" I stammered, and a genuine shock ran through my body.

"You know," said Ronnie, "a piece of birthday cake. We're celebrating all the January birthdays in the shop today. There's plenty of cake. Why don't you come on over and have some?"

I stood up on shaky legs and assured Ronnie that I would visit the shop in a few minutes for some cake. He smiled and left, and as the tears began streaming down my face, I silently gave thanks for the chance to celebrate Will's birthday.

I knew deep within that this was no coincidence.

And I know deep within that if we will remain open, the help, guidance, and love we need are there for all of us. This is true in your search experience, too. Moment by moment, messages and help are streaming in. What is offering itself to you at the moment?

Today's Spiritual Guideline

Write in your journal about something that has happened in your search recently that initially appeared to be a coincidence but later proved to be of assistance to you on the journey.

Write yourself a promise that, in the day ahead, you will pay special attention to all the "coincidences" in your life!

50 *Flow*

Flow.
Sometimes called the Zone,
it's the place I want to be,

In reality, I cannot find it —
it will find me,
if I allow it.

Today I will
turn off the internal chatter
slow things down,
find that break in space and time
and allow the flow to pick me up
and carry me away.

Today's Spiritual Guideline

Practice flowing. In the day ahead, you might wish to start simply, by flowing with the traffic as you drive — or by flowing with the movement of the people around you on the bus or train — instead of internally fighting with what is happening around you.

At a more advanced level, see if you can detect and synchronize yourself with the flow of a meeting with someone or an interview. Actively participate and learn, without being concerned about the pace or progress of events.

At the end of the day, write in your journal one experience you had of "going with the flow." How did you feel at the time? What was the outcome of practicing being at ease? Would you benefit from some more practice? What might you want to do to continue the flow?

5 | *Hope*

I don't know what may come tomorrow,
but I know something will be provided for me today.

It seems that when I am the most afraid,
hope shows up in the most surprising places.

All I have to do is let it in.

Sometimes my stubborn streak closes doors
and refuses to let love come through.
I want to be self-sufficient, disconnected,
when I know I really am connected to a greater plan.

This day I will remember:
I will meet people who can meet my needs —
even needs I don't recognize.
I will find help in ways I don't expect.
I will trust that I am not alone in this search.

Today's Spiritual Guideline

Consider this thought: *"I have a spiritual interconnection with everything."*

Spend some time reflecting on these ideas:
- The land and I are connected.
- The weather and I are connected.
- The birds and I are connected.
- The people I encounter on this search and I are connected.

Write in your journal how your sense of interconnectedness helps you see that you are provided for and gives you hope in the ambiguity of the job search.

52 *People Are Sent*

The people who can assist you with your sacred purpose often enter and exit your life just when they are needed. You may not always recognize them, but if you can open your awareness to them, you may find true helpers in unexpected guises.

Recently I was driving through south Georgia in the midst of a tropical storm. Visibility on the highway was poor, and my windshield wipers were working overtime trying to keep up with the driving rain.

Suddenly I heard a pop, and my driver's-side wiper was hanging uselessly to the left of its normal arc. I was abruptly blinded. I pulled to the side of the highway and attempted to diagnose the problem. But the rain and wind were so heavy I couldn't see. So I got back in the car and limped along to the next exit.

I drove into a gas station and was trying in vain to find what had broken in the wiper linkage when a man in a pickup truck, someone with a day's growth of beard, asked what the problem was. While I was explaining the situation to him, my wife retrieved an older man, toothless and looking a bit sleepy, from within the station. There was no mechanic on duty, he told us, but he thought he might be able to help.

Somehow, between the two of them, they immediately found the problem: a loose nut where the drive linkage attached to the wiper arm. The man from the pickup truck produced a crescent wrench, the older man tightened and adjusted the nut into its proper position, and they both disappeared back into the station. After a delay of less than five minutes, we were on our way again.

They had emerged precisely when we needed them. Although it initially seemed that they were not the right people for the job, it turned out that they were *exactly* the ones who were needed.

The people who are needed in your life are present. They have something of significance to contribute to the fulfillment of your life's purpose. Your part of the process is to pay attention so you don't miss them!

Today's Spiritual Guideline

Try this in the day ahead: Each time you meet a person, remind yourself that she or he is sent to you for a reason, that the people who come into your life this day have something to offer.

At the end of the day, review the events that took place. Who helped you when you weren't expecting it? Who gave you information that surprised you? Write the details in your journal and give special thanks for those people.

53 *Networking*

Everyone has a network. We can't live without one. Yet I often hear people on job search say, "But I don't have a network."

You may have had such thoughts yourself. The problem isn't in your lack of network; it's in your *definition* of network. If you think of network only in terms of "who can get or give me a job," that limits the possibilities. Think instead of the deep, wide network that helps and maintains your life: parents, siblings, partner, spouse, the grocer, the mail carrier, friends, co-workers, supervisors, teachers, ministers, counselors, therapists, physicians, service people, drivers, groundskeepers, the exterminator . . . *the exterminator???*

A few years ago, I was assisting a man who had lost his job as a maintenance engineer in a factory. He lived in a small town, and he was convinced that his job-search networking opportunities were extremely limited in that town.

One afternoon he found himself at home without much to do, his search process stagnating a bit. The exterminator arrived to perform the monthly maintenance, and, while spraying around the baseboards, he commented to the out-of-work engineer that he had never seen him at home at this hour before. My client explained that he had lost his job through a downsizing and was hoping to get into a certain plant, but that he really didn't know anyone there.

The exterminator stopped in mid-spray and stood upright with a bit of a smile on his face. "I've treated that plant for bugs for years, and the plant manager and I are good friends. We play golf and go to dinner together nearly every week. Let me introduce you to him."

Ask and you shall receive. Knock and the door shall be opened. Seek and you shall find.

Each and every person you know is a potential link to someone you don't know, a link to the persons who can assist you or take you where you need to go. Those links will lead you not only to jobs, but also to wisdom or spiritual figures who will be of great value to you throughout your life.

Today's Spiritual Guideline

Consider this: *"There is a person in my network who will be of immense value to my personal and professional development, but I have not yet recognized that person."*

Write in your journal the name of a person in your daily or weekly network of contacts whom you have never considered particularly valuable to your job search. During the day ahead, approach that person and tell her or him what you are trying to accomplish in this search. Listen to the response with care and attentiveness.

Record the key points of your encounter in your journal. What action will you take or what contacts will you make based on what this person said to you?

54 Networking and Relationship

Networking is most effective when it is viewed as relationship building. It is much richer and deeper than simply going to a party and handing out business cards, asking about job openings, or asking for specific favors. Networking has a deeper spiritual quality when it includes both giving and receiving, meeting the genuine needs of everyone involved.

Spiritually-based networking happens when giving — without expectation of specific return — exists on both sides of the relationship. As you talk to people in your network, be aware of what *their* needs are in the relationship. Open your mind and your heart to what you can do for them. Perhaps they need simple friendship, or a person to talk to, or assistance with a specific project. At times, this may require listening carefully to what is not said, as well as to what is said.

Even if it appears on the surface that you can't satisfy any of the person's needs, you may be able to refer him or her to someone who can help. And even if all you can offer is caring and concern in the spirit of deep connectedness, you may be giving that person exactly what he or she needs in the present moment.

At our spiritual core, all of humanity — indeed all of creation — is one. We are social beings, living in relationship with all other humans. We are meant to help and assist one another. To fail to utilize the assistance of others is to close ourselves off from their and our full potential.

We are called to radical openness in all of our relationships, and this is particularly important in our job search network.

Today's Spiritual Guideline

Make a conscious decision for the day ahead to temporarily put aside your personal concerns and concentrate on the concerns of someone whom you meet.

Listen closely and carefully to the person's problems or challenges or ideas and respond to their need in that moment.

At the end of the day, reflect in your journal on the gifts you have received from focusing on someone else's issues.

55 *Seeing People*

This morning as I was driving to the office, I noticed something: The cars whizzing by me were only cars, behaving in sometimes-unpredictable ways. At times, they were simply other presences. At other times, they seemed threatening and dangerous.

I consciously raised my gaze. Lo and behold, there were people driving those cars! Real human beings! I began to notice their faces. Lots of frowns, lots of apparent stress and worry. Occasionally, these were punctuated by someone smiling, laughing, or simply wearing an expression of peace or joy.

I observed each person for perhaps only a second. Certainly no more than that. And yet, when I paid attention and looked at each one, I learned. I learned that these were real people, not just machines shoving up against one another in the busy traffic. I saw that each person had their own internal world.

As you move through your search in the day ahead, remember that you are meeting people, not the roles, jobs, or machines with which they surround themselves. Raise your gaze to their faces and pay attention. Notice. Listen.

In this spirit of openness, you may be surprised at the new information and wisdom you take in. What you learn from each person will help you in finding the fulfillment of your purpose.

Today's Spiritual Guideline

Make a list in your journal of the people whom you will be seeing in the day ahead. Instead of focusing on what you want or need from them, make a note of something you'd like to learn from or about each person. See what happens . . .

At the end of the day, note in your journal what you observed or heard that touches on your current job-search needs. Give thanks for each person you met.

56 *Honest Questions*

We are all in community. That is both a gift and a fact of human life.

While it is always appropriate to consult our inner life, at the same time it is appropriate to consult the collective wisdom of the community in which we find ourselves. And, usually, if we ask honest questions and really listen to the responses, we are given the guidance we need at the moment.

What is an honest question?

It is a question that does not beg for or lead the responder to a particular, predetermined response. It is a specific question that allows the responder to go deep into his or her spiritual core and give an honest answer. It is a question that is radically open to the possibilities; it does not judge and it does not assume. The honest question does not ask for a specific job; it allows for a job to develop out of the natural sharing of information that stays focused on one's central purpose and mission.

But there's one thing you need to know about honest questions: The answers you receive may not be what you expect. The information may not lead immediately to a specific job.

Your part of the ongoing process is to trust that the wisdom of your community is part of what will ultimately lead you to the work that is waiting for you.

Today's Spiritual Guideline

Write an honest question you would like to explore with someone in your network, a question that is fundamentally open to a spontaneous, not a predetermined, answer. Within the next few days, ask the person this question. Listen carefully and without judgment, and record in your journal what you hear.

Consider the response to your question meditatively and give thanks for the wisdom that has been shared with you.

57 *Lessons from People*

All of the people who come into my life today
are meant to be there.
Every person I see today matters.
Each has something to offer.
Each has something to teach me.

Let me pause to consider
the lessons that each encounter can give
as I seek out my purpose.

In every quiet moment of the day,
let me silently hear and listen to
the guidance and the help that are being offered to me.

Let me slide into that place
where the love of the Universe
and my heart's desire intersect
to do the work I was sent to do.

Today's Spiritual Guideline

Consider this: *"All of the people I have met, or will meet, today belong exactly where they are. Each person has a lesson for me now."*

Practice seeing the value in every person you meet in the day ahead. As you are talking to each person, let the thought surface to your mind, *"This person matters."*

At the end of the day, record in your journal how this approach affected you. Think particularly about persons who annoyed or challenged you. Why do you think they came into your life at this time? What did they have to teach you? Reflect upon and write about how these lessons might be applied to your search.

58 *Writing*

Some say that the writing of letters is a lost art. And so it is. Telephones, fax machines, and e-mail seem to have made the old-fashioned paper-letter obsolete.

Consider for a moment the spiritual value of writing letters in the course of your job search.

As people appear in your life to provide you with wisdom and information, to direct you along the path of your purpose, you can gratefully acknowledge their gifts. True, a telephone call is a wonderful way to say thank you. But it is not the only way, and in many cases it is not the best way.

When you put your thanksgiving on a piece of paper, you give your thoughts a kind of permanence. The recipient of your letter can feel its texture, hold it in their hands. They can read it again and again. They can store it in an instantly retrievable form, no high technology required.

To write a letter means to take the time to care. Writing implies that you value this individual and his or her contribution above the level of the ordinary. You recognize and honor the guidance and wisdom that have been freely given.

We all, at the deepest level, want to give gifts of great value. In the act of writing, you can give and receive a spiritual gift. You get a chance to build a deeper connection with another; they get a chance to feel valued and appreciated.

Today's Spiritual Guideline

Take some quiet moments to consider people who have been helpful to you recently. Chose one person to whom you would especially like to send your thanks. Let them know in writing. Be specific as to the kind of help or wisdom you have received from this person. Include your genuine thanks that this person is a part of your life.

59 *Discernment*

I have done all the personal assessments.

I have examined what I do well
and what I most like to do.

I have narrowed it down.

I have begun to speak to people in my network,
and I have listened carefully to them.

I have documented it all.
I have synthesized the documents, and
I have carefully studied the results.

But I'm still not sure what to do.

Where is my answer?

The discernment of wisdom
is in the listening,
in the hearing of the whispering,
the quiet whispering that knows.

"Listen," a small inner voice reminds me.
"Listen to the silence deep inside."

The answer is there.

And — surprise! —
the answer today
may be different from the answer last week or next year.

Today's Spiritual Guideline

Take some quiet time to listen to yourself. What are you whispering to yourself that you haven't heard before?

Use your journal today to describe precisely how you are feeling about your job search at this point in the journey. What are you apprehensive about? What are you excited about? If there is something you have been thinking about doing, or asking, or investigating for a while but have put it off, make note of it. Ask yourself if this is the time to take action on it.

60 Creation

Employment ads often state that they are looking for someone who is "results oriented." Translation: "someone who can make a great deal of money."

There is absolutely nothing wrong with making money. But here's the secret: The process of finding a wonderful job, or of making a great deal of money, is always the same — something from nothing.

Nothing is the ground of all that is. Everything that is, was, and will be comes out of nothing.

Nothingness is the ultimate ground of creativity. It is the blank canvas upon which we, as artists, will create our masterpieces. The masterpiece of your career is created out of nothing as well.

So if you find yourself worried because the "right" job just isn't coming your way, stop struggling and give "nothing" a chance to work its magic.

When it seems that nothing very productive is happening, this is precisely the time to cherish the moment. Go deep inside and seek the waiting silence of nothing. That is the central point of creation. When you are in touch with this place of beginning, you are in touch with the source of all creation. When you are immersed in the process of creating something from nothing, you are linked with all creation.

Think on this.

Today's Spiritual Guideline

Today, open your journal to the next blank page. Spend time meditating on the blankness of the page. What does it look like? What does it feel like? What does it suggest to you?

Now, allow your mind to become as blank as that page. You may find it hard to stay "blank" for very long. Outside thoughts may intrude. Each time an idea or concern crosses your mind, calmly let it wash over you, as a wave of water. Then, as the wave recedes, return to the still, quiet place of the blank page.

Leave this page in your journal blank. Return to it whenever you are feeling less than productive, when you are fresh out of ideas, when you are running on empty. Use it to remind yourself that all creation starts with nothing.

6 | *Information*

This is an excellent time in your job search for what I call an "Information Meeting." An Information Meeting is any time you spend getting specific information about a particular job or career field or company by speaking directly with the person or persons who have some information to offer you.

The secret here is not to limit your inquiry to a specific job in a specific organization. You are usually better off if you avoid asking the question: "Do you know of any openings?" This will limit the discussion and close down any ongoing dialogue. Once that topic is exhausted, there is nothing more to talk about.

Another common problem with Information Meetings is that many people approach them already envisioning what they will receive from the encounter. It is important to plan the agenda beforehand, to consider and write down the career and job-related issues you need specific information about. However, don't fall into the trap of planning the way the meeting will go! Your plan may not be the way it *needs* to go. Your spiritual practice will assist you in maintaining a sense of openness to all possibilities.

Finally, when you arrange an Information Meeting, cultivate an openness to being in relationship. Remind yourself that you are there both to give and receive. Focus on entering the flow of the relationship, with a sense of give and take.

Recognize that this is a meeting for the sharing of wisdom. Recognize it as a sacred event in the course of your life. Remember that each and every encounter will be transformative in some way. Each and every encounter will help you focus your mission.

Today's Spiritual Guideline

What are the questions on your mind? What information do you need to further your job search? List your questions in your journal.

Now create a list of possible people who might have this information.

Select one person from your list to call today and make an appointment. Be clear with them that you are seeking information, not a specific job.

In your journal, write the name of the person with whom you will be meeting. Keep this person in your sphere of attention this week.

Start a list of specific questions that you want to ask this person and build on your list during the time between today and your meeting.

Finally, write a commitment to yourself in your journal that you will not pre-plan the results of this Information Meeting, that you will go with an open heart and mind to receive what is offered.

62 *Uncertainty*

I don't know what this means.
I just met with a person who gave me
lots of information.
Some of it I knew or suspected,
some of it was a surprise.
I don't know what this means.

Does it call my objective into question?
Does it make me face new facts?
Does it add something new?
Is it right or wrong?
Will it lead me in my career?
Will it turn into something I can use?

I don't know.
Good.

I give myself the quiet space
to let it settle down,
to find my center and grow quieter.
Then I can consider what it might mean.

I may learn something I didn't know.
Good.
I may make a connection I never made before.
Good.
I may meet a new person.
Good.
I may serve myself and others as a result of this information.
Good.

I don't know what this means.
How fortunate for me!

Today's Spiritual Guideline

Think of something you learned today, or in recent days, that has left you feeling confused or uncertain.

Take a few minutes to see this uncertainty in a new light — as a gift of great value, as an opportunity to open to something new.

In your journal, write a prayer, meditation, or poem honoring uncertainty as a friend and thanking it for the hidden gifts it brings.

63 *Humor*

Lest all this honest questioning and searching and uncertainty get you down, there's another important part of the job search I want to remind you about: humor.

You may notice that you just haven't had much to smile about in a long time. Consider this: It is your natural state to be happy and to laugh. Yes. Your natural state.

And, just as there are people out there in your network to help you with specifics in your job or career search, so are there also people to assist you with getting back in touch with the silly side of life. Open yourself to the possibilities: movies, videos, television, magazines, books, newspapers, comics, comedy clubs, and on and on — they can be an integral and vital part of the "light side" of your life.

As part of your spiritual practice, ask to be directed to the presence of teachers of the funny and the humorous. Ask for the help you need to lighten up.

There is no more deeply spiritual act than to laugh out of deep, inner joy.

Today's Spiritual Guideline

Think of humorous or silly encounters you have had during your job search. And if you've already started to respond, "There's nothing funny in this," think again! Don't dig for profound messages; simply allow yourself the chance to smile.

Jot down in your journal any humorous situations, actions, and statements that come to mind. Share some of these humorous moments with a friend.

Make a special agreement with yourself that, during the day ahead, you will pay attention to the small things that make you smile — a child's giggle, a pet's antics, a colleague's jokes.

64 *Thanksgiving*

I have done a good job this day in peace and in confidence.
I have followed the process and been faithful to my objective.
I have talked to people
who have graciously shared their wisdom with me.
I have entered and enjoyed the flow of life.
I have laughed and enjoyed the adventure.

For all of this and more, I give thanks.
Help me to give in the same full measure
as I have received this day.

Today's Spiritual Guideline

You may be in a place where this reflection fits you perfectly
. . . or, you may be in a place where "thanksgiving" seems
very far from your mood.

Wherever you are on the continuum of ups and downs, take some time
today to name in your journal at least one thing that you are thankful for
today — even if it is something simple, such as being able to walk in the
sun, or being able to talk to someone who cares about you, or having a
few moments of calming time for yourself. No experience is too small
for thanks. And no discouragement is too big to negate pleasure.

One way of giving thanks is to contribute some beauty to the world you
live in. It may mean cleaning out the garage or straightening out that mess
on your desk. It may mean planting something in your garden or hanging
something you like to look at on your wall. Write in your journal one thing
you will do in the day ahead to make your thanks "visible" by adding a bit
of beauty to your life.

65 *Classified Ads*

Most job hunters study the "Help Wanted" ads. And while some jobs are found that way, the percentage of successful results per individual is somewhere around fifteen percent or even less. So do you even need to use this source of information?

In the context of the spiritual job search, the answer is yes. Keep the following in mind:

The ads may or may not lead you to the specific job that is right for you, but they will act as stepping stones. They may lead you in the direction of persons or opportunities that will ultimately take you where you need to be. And they will always bring new learnings.

Approach the classified ads with a reverent heart, as you approach all the tasks of the job search. Before reading them, spend time in meditation and prayer. Become centered and silent. Then, review the objective you have set for yourself. Consider not only the specific objective, but the spirit of it as well.

As you read the ads, ask yourself the following questions:

- Is this job consistent with my stated objective?
- Will this job help me accomplish my mission, serve the purpose I see for myself on this Earth?
- In all honesty, do I have the appropriate qualifications for this position?
- Is the job located where I want to be?
- What other information do I need concerning this position?
- Do I know anyone either inside or outside this organization who can give me more information about this job?
- Should I respond to this ad?
- What would be the best way to respond?

For each ad that looks like a potential for you, honestly answer these questions for yourself. If you are faithful to the spiritual approach, you will be guided to the path that is right for you.

Today's Spiritual Guideline

I'm going to make a radical suggestion: As part of your spiritual practice, commit to this spiritual focus on the classified ads for the next two weeks.

After reviewing the ads each day, choose one as a subject for your reflection. Ask yourself the questions I've outlined above. Use your journal to record your responses. Make particular note of ways in which this ad appears to match, or not match, your identified objective.

The point here is not necessarily to get a job from one of these ads, but rather to practice the art of testing to see how various job opportunities fit your objective.

66 *Interviews*

You've been to interviews before and you will be interviewed again. You probably have specific things you do ahead of an interview, such as reviewing the questions that might be asked, reviewing your career objectives, practicing with a friend or career counselor, gathering information about the company that is interviewing you, planning the practical matters such as dress, transportation, and logistics, and so on. All of these are worthy pursuits as you prepare to interview. All are prerequisites to a successful interview.

Yet the spiritually-based job search suggests some other preparation as well. Getting centered and touching the silence within are keys to staying focused. You can use your daily spiritual practice to do this, but I also suggest adding a specific meditation process just prior to the ritual of the interview.

Start with a moment of silence. Give thanks in advance for the opportunity to learn and experience the interview. Ask to be given the wisdom to see and understand the lessons that will be given. Give thanks for the sacred presence of your mentors, friends, or career counselors who may have helped you find this place. Finish by expressing your openness to and gratitude for the messages and lessons that will be revealed during the interview.

If, during the course of the questions and answers of the interview, you find yourself growing anxious, briefly and silently return to your inner quiet. Remind yourself that all you need is provided, that you have prepared well for this experience.

If you have an urge to try and make sense of everything that is happening in the interview, to analyze it as it is happening, resist that urge. It may be several hours, days, or weeks later that meanings and lessons are revealed. Allow yourself to be at peace with the process.

After the interview, continue your spiritual practice. In meditation and prayer, give thanks for this opportunity and time of learning. Give thanks for and bless the new people who have come into your life through this interview.

Remind yourself that, though this ultimately may or may not be the job within which you can live out your purpose, the experience of the interview is of great value. Give thanks .

Today's Spiritual Guideline

I want to share with you something that I've found helpful.

Here is a brief meditation that you can write on a small card, carry in your purse or wallet, and take a quiet moment to read just before you meet with your interviewer:

As I prepare to speak with this person,
grant us both wisdom.
Give me the ability to hear clearly
what is said and what is not said.
Remind me that this time together
is a lesson.
Learning is everywhere.

No one has a monopoly on the truth;
it comes in bits and pieces.
Help me this day to receive and accept
precisely those bits of the truth that I need.

67 Listening

Every person has a story.
We have only to listen
and the experiences and wisdom of a lifetime
are available to us.

Our part is to be quiet and still,
and resist the urge to "one-up" them;
They will tell us what we need to know
and more.

The beauty of this is that
we don't need to go chasing after the world.
It reveals itself in every moment.
It reveals itself in every person.

We get into trouble
when we try to force it
down some predetermined path we have thought.

Help me in this moment to enter the flow
and benefit from it.
Help me to withhold judgment
and trust in the working out of it all.

Today's Spiritual Guideline

In the day ahead, practice your listening skills with everyone you speak with. Think of it as great practice for future interviews!

Get clarification if you are not sure what point is being made. *"What did she say? What did she mean?"* Ask her.

Don't impose your own preconceptions. *"Did I just make a conclusion about something that wasn't said?"* Keep listening to what is being said.

Don't pre-judge the value of what you are hearing. *"Oh, that would never work for me."* Keep an open mind.

Don't do all the talking — either out loud or with that quiet little voice inside of your head. Leave room for new information to come in.

At the end of the day, record in your journal the things you heard this day that you want to come back to and consider at another time.

68 *The "No" Experience*

Somewhere along the line it's going to happen — somebody is going to say "no." Probably more than once.

"We've selected someone more in line with our requirements."

"I don't believe we've got a good match here."

"You were certainly in the running, and we sincerely appreciate your interest, but we have selected another candidate."

And on and on.

Will you feel badly? Probably yes.

Might you have a bad day or a bruised ego? Probably yes.

Is it the end of the world or the demise of your search? Certainly not.

In quiet contemplation, allow yourself to have the feelings of disappointment or hurt. Don't deny them; they are real. Honor them. Feel them thoroughly. It hurts to be turned down. Then allow your feelings to slowly dissolve into a calm silence. Now is the time to seek your inner teacher. The "no" experience has something to teach you, something very important, something that is going to move your search forward. The lesson is uniquely yours if you can listen inwardly for the message.

The lesson might include:

- This is not my path. This is not the direction for me to take as I seek to live out my purpose.
- There is something better or more appropriate out there for me, something that more closely fulfills my purpose. I will continue my spiritual practice so that I will recognize it and be able to respond when it happens.
- I did not, for whatever reason, communicate my enthusiasm or ability to perform in the position.
- This potential employer was not prepared to hear and receive my message. He or she was in a different place, and it was not possible to communicate effectively at this time.

- I need to honestly and deeply reconsider my objective. It may be an objective of striving and struggle, rather than an expression of my mission and purpose. Perhaps my campaign is in need of a tune-up, or it may be in need of a totally new direction. I will devote quiet consideration to this issue.

You might not be able to discern the precise lesson in the short term. But you can trust that the "no" experience, like every other experience, can be a valued teacher and friend. Allow yourself to have the feelings associated with it and to cultivate an honest openness to the lessons it contains.

Today's Spiritual Guideline

Think of two encounters you have had recently — one that went well and one that did not produce the desired or expected result.

Compare and contrast the two in your journal. What did you learn from each? Identify the needs that were either met or not met for both of you in the encounter.

As honestly as possible, identify and write in your journal what you learned from each encounter.

69 *Refusal*

This person brushed me off.
And yet, there is a learning here.

Help me to see it.
Help me to break through
and see beyond the wall I have built with my pride.

There is a lesson.
There is always a lesson.

Perhaps this is telling me
to be more compassionate,
to listen more carefully.

Perhaps this is showing me
how not to behave
when someone else asks me for help.

Perhaps this is showing me
there is another path for me.

Perhaps this is teaching me
the lesson of patience,
the lesson of waiting.

There is a lesson here.
Help me to get it now.

Today's Spiritual Guideline

Think of someone you are having difficulty obtaining access to, perhaps someone you would like to include in your network or someone who may be a potential employer.

Write about this person in your journal, describing the obstacles or problems you are facing.

Take a quiet moment and consider the lessons these difficulties suggest to you.

70 The Nature of Careers

At one time, the words "career" and "job" were nearly synonymous.

I think of my father who, in the late 1940s following a brief stint in the Navy during the closing months of World War Two, secured a position with a company in Nashville. He stayed there over forty years before he retired. He had a long-term and enduring relationship with this relatively small, family-owned business, and Dad became an integral part of the company, a member of the family both figuratively and literally.

This scenario is no longer the norm. Today such careers are the exception. We have become a society of nomads, occupying, on average, some seven to ten jobs throughout the course of a lifetime. (A possible exception might be professions such as medicine and the law, although even in these fields there is a greater fluctuation and change than ever before.) We are even beginning to see the rise of multiple jobs, or missions, held simultaneously.

Yet even though the nature of careers has changed dramatically, the way many of us conceive of careers has not kept pace.

This might be an excellent time to give yourself an internal spring-cleaning. Clean out the dusty corners where the old beliefs of the "way it used to be" have accumulated. Open the windows to the fresh air of new possibilities.

If you have been searching for *THE* job — the one that will enable you to perform the mission that directly fulfills your purpose — consider other alternatives. You could hold serial jobs, a sequence of assignments that will meet your needs and the needs of those you serve. Or you could fulfill multiple missions simultaneously with several assignments or tasks ongoing at the same time.

This is not to suggest that you take on more than you can handle! The spiritual job search beckons us to live responsibly, caring for ourselves as well as others.

What it does suggest is an openness to the nontraditional. One job for your lifetime may not be your way. One job at a time may not even be your way. The traditional work sites may not be your way. Part of your spiritual path is to explore the wide range of choices open to you.

Today's Spiritual Guideline

Start your quiet time today by taking at least five deep breaths. Each time you inhale, feel yourself opening to a wider vision of "job." Each time you exhale, let yourself rest in the assurance that your work in the world is waiting for you.

Set aside a section in your journal and label it "Alternatives." Begin to seek out information on nontraditional options — through newspaper and magazine articles, articles on the Web, information from other people — and list the ones that spark an interest in you.

As you collect ideas for alternative possibilities, compare them with your developing statement of objective. Use your daily spiritual practice to quietly and meditatively consider these possibilities.

7 | *Many Second Chances*

One of the most central — and hardest to accept — ideas I keep mentioning is that every experience of our lives has learning value. *Every* experience.

There is something to be learned in the brushing of our teeth.

There is something to be learned in the behavior of the traffic and our response to it.

There is something to be learned in every aspect of the job search, as it is happening, whether or not it leads to the actual acquisition of a job. If you interview for a job but don't get it, there is a lesson in it — if you are open to the learning value of the experience. And each lesson will move you in a positive direction toward where you need to be, job and career-wise.

I keep saying this — and assuring you of this — because it is so vitally important in your job hunting. There are always second, third, fourth, fifth, and more chances. And there are always more lessons to be learned.

Today's Spiritual Guideline

Some lessons keep appearing in our lives. They may take the form of repeated pleasant — or unpleasant — experiences.

Today, take an inventory of events or experiences that seem to repeat in your life, especially in career or job-related situations. Note the most frequently repeating type of event. Give yourself some time to reflect on this.

What do you perceive to be the lesson or lessons contained in this type of situation? What do you think is being presented to you? What are you learning? Record your thoughts in your journal.

72 *Order*

This search has a life of its own.

As I look back over my notes,
my schedules, my contacts, and
all the lessons and directions that have come my way,
I realize this job search has literally taken on a life of its own.
The pieces of the search are part of an ongoing whole.

That is the flow, the organic nature of life.
That is, in fact, life —
order emerges from seeming chaos.

It happens every day,
but I don't usually see it.

Today I will recognize my part in the larger flow of life,
the order that seems to appear out of nowhere
but actually appears from everywhere.

I am part of the natural flow of life,
and my part is to learn what I can from it
and enjoy the journey.

Today's Spiritual Guideline

Take some time today to look back over your journal. Pay particular attention to any recurring themes that seem to emerge. Note any themes you become aware of on a new journal page.

What do these themes tell you about the natural order, the natural flow of your life? What feelings do you have about the themes that are appearing?

Record your responses and end with a thanksgiving that you are part of a larger Creation.

73 *The Pursuit*

As you pursue this spiritual path, specific jobs will become available to approach and compete for. In fact, the quantity of potential jobs may ultimately surprise you: You may never have imagined that so many diverse opportunities would be available to you.

The question will then arise: Which ones should I pursue and which should I release?

Turn to your spiritual practice. Once again, there are lessons to be learned.

This may be a confusing place for you — no one can advise you with certainty as to the best course for you. But you have inner and outer resources. Use your spiritual practice to help you get a clear, undistorted view of the possibilities. Go to a quiet place internally and listen for your inner wisdom. Use your friends and mentors and community to give you feedback. And, perhaps most importantly, compare the options in front of you with your own objectives and mission and purpose.

When you do decide to pursue a particular job, you can eat up countless hours second-guessing yourself, and it will get you nowhere. Once you have reached a decision in quiet, move forward in peace and confidence. You will be shown the way. Trust that the work with your name on it is finding you.

Today's Spiritual Guideline

In your journal, list the job opportunities that you are developing and that may become available to you at this time.

Spend some quiet time considering this list in the light of your objectives, mission, and purpose.

Then make a commitment for today: Select two opportunities that you want to actively pursue. And before you scare yourself with the idea of "commitment," remember that you are committing to learning what these opportunities have to teach you!

Give thanks for the experiences you will have as you pursue these options.

A Special Note

As you approach the end of this book, I obviously don't know where you are in your job-search process. So I am going to close our time together by offering two different paths:

- *Meditations 74-78* are especially useful if you are discouraged in your job search;

- *Meditations 79-83* are helpful if you have been offered a job.

You may even find yourself in *both* states at the same time, if the job you are being offered is not one that you envisioned for yourself! Select the meditations that fit for you. Remember: Both states are an important part of the process. Whatever is presenting itself to you — whether it is a continued search or a decision — whatever it is, it is a gift.

74 *Gifts*

All is given to you.
Your life is given to you.
Your mission is a gift.
Your friends are gifts.
Your enemies are gifts.
The Earth is a gift.
Your feelings are gifts.
Your possessions are gifts.
Your family is a gift.
Your children are gifts.
Your life is a gift.

Today's Spiritual Guideline

What gifts have you received in the last twenty-four hours?

If you are tempted to answer that question with a quick, "None," I challenge you to think again. Even if a "gift" seems to be a negative one, such as someone turning you down, there is still the gift of a lesson in it. And, I believe that if you sit in silence for a few more minutes, you will be able to think of a positive gift you have received as well — perhaps someone's touch of a hand, or a smile directed at you, or a piece of information you did not have before.

In your journal, write down each gift you can think of, without judging its value.

Write your thoughts of gratitude; you might want to put them in the form of a prayer or poem. If some person has given you a special gift today, you might want to send the giver a letter of thanks.

75 *Emptiness*

Sometimes I'm running dry.

Nothing will come.
I'm fresh out of ideas.

And so I turn to the quiet inner silence,
the source of my being,
the center that gives me my mission
and enables me to fulfill my purpose.

Today's Spiritual Guideline

Give yourself a chance literally to "run on empty" for a while. Give yourself permission to have no plans, no strategy for this space of time.

Go into silence and think of nothing. When a stray thought intrudes, picture your mind as a blank slate from which any thought can be erased. Stay in this state for as long as you wish.

Now permit yourself to have random thoughts. Take out your journal and write them down, having no concern for their meaningfulness or relevance to anything. Write until you feel you can write no longer.

Read what you have written. What actions do these seemingly random thoughts suggest?

76 *Depression*

Today, I am most assuredly depressed.

For the last couple of days,
I have neglected my network,
forgotten my objective,
felt the fear,
wallowed in self-pity.
I have let my spiritual practice slide.

And yet, I know it is all a learning.

Help me to see the lessons here —
to feel the worry and fear,
admit it,
then let it go.

To take my hands off the steering wheel,
to permit the Universe to direct me
on the path toward fulfilling my sacred purpose.

I will continue to trust that the guidance
and help I need
are ever available and ready.

Teach me to learn in the quiet moments.

Today's Spiritual Guideline

This is a good time to go back and re-read the letter you wrote for your first journal entry in this book (see page 9).

Review the commitment you made to finding your sacred purpose in life. Give yourself some inner quiet time to reconnect with your commitment.

Review what you wrote about your fears and excitements for the journey. What do you want to add to this today?

Write a "response" letter to yourself, as if you were an outside mentor giving support. Congratulate yourself for the work you have done so far, name some of the gifts and lessons you have received along the way, and reaffirm your intention to continue seeking your sacred purpose in life.

77 *Sorrow*

I was once mighty,
riding on top of the world,

And then I found that
my desk had been cleaned out for me.

There is a hard, painful lesson here.

Give me the quiet, the space,
the peace to learn what it is.

Allow me to feel this sorrow
and understand what it is saying.

I know I can and will
move on to other places.

But for today, I need quiet
to begin to believe
that a miracle is
possible in my life.

Today's Spiritual Guideline

Think of an experience, in either the recent or distant past, in which you had a sudden loss of job or status. (If this has never happened to you, give thanks and ponder how you would respond if it ever did.)

- How did you deal with it?
- What resources were you able to draw on for help?
- Who stepped forward to offer assistance, support, comfort, and reassurance?

Record in your journal, in detail, what seemed most helpful at that time.

Consider which of these might be helpful at this time. Note in writing what resources — both internal and external — you can draw on now.

78 *Paralysis*

I haven't done much on my job campaign in a while.

It is time to do something —
anything.
I've got to do something,
even if it's "wrong."

Yet, if in honesty, truth, integrity,
and through my prayers and meditations,
my actions are what I know
I have been led to do,
I trust that I am doing what is right for me.

I will do what I am called to do this day.

Today's Spiritual Guideline

Share with a trusted friend or mentor your experience of feeling "stuck." Listen carefully to the words of that trusted one.

Either at the time of the interaction or shortly thereafter, record in your journal as faithfully as possible that person's thoughts.

Reflect on these thoughts as part of your spiritual practice today.

79 *The Offer*

A job has been offered
just when I least expected it!
I'm surprised.
But I'm not surprised.

This is the radical ambiguity of the spiritual process,
A rational event — I have been working hard for this!
An irrational event — it seems to have come out of nowhere.

I am reminded:
Ask and you shall receive.
Knock and the door shall be opened.

Sometimes,
deeply embedded in the quiet,
comes what I have sought.

I know why I am here.
I trust what I understand my sacred purpose to be.
Now is the time to act.

The doors are open
and the way is made clear.
The time has come.

Today's Spiritual Guideline

Give yourself some generous time for reflection today, giving thanks for the opportunity that has been offered. Do not attempt at this early stage to formulate a course of action. Simply and quietly give thanks.

Following this time of thanksgiving, record in your journal all that excites and concerns you about this offer. Then put your journal aside and go into silence for as long as you need.

80 *The Consideration*

They have offered me a job,
and I'm not sure how to proceed.

I know I need to negotiate
something.

I shouldn't just accept the first offer
they make.

Should I?

The thoughts are roaring through my head
too fast to comprehend.

I choose to slow them down.

I voluntarily interrupt myself
and enter the silence
of meditation
where the issues can begin to fall into place.

Today's Spiritual Guideline

Begin your reflective time again today with a thanksgiving for the job that has been offered.

Now take a few minutes to go back and read your most recent objective statement carefully. Record in your journal how much the present offer matches — or doesn't match — your stated objective.

Begin two lists: REASONS TO ACCEPT and REASONS NOT TO ACCEPT. Keep adding to these lists until you are comfortable that you have exhausted the possibilities.

Then set your lists aside and go into deep silence for as long as you can, preferably about an hour.

Return to the two lists and read them again. What is the next step you think you need to take to resolve any outstanding questions you still have? Make a commitment to yourself in writing to seek out the information you require.

8 | *The Decision*

Many job-search guides advise you to do some decision-making exercises, such as listing all the pros and cons of a job on a sheet of paper and seeing how they weigh out. And so you should; such an exercise can be exceedingly helpful in the decision-making process.

Some sources also recommend checking the offer presented against a list of your personal needs to see if a match exists. Again, you should do this.

Others suggest that you go back to your objective to see how well it is met by the offer. Do this, too.

But, ultimately, I urge you to return to your spiritual practice of meditation and prayer. Go deep within as you have before and ask to be granted the wisdom to make this decision.

This wisdom may come in different forms. It may be a direct answer, a direct knowing of the direction you should take. It may be encouragement to seek out the opinion of another, perhaps someone you consulted earlier as part of your networking process. It may be a referral to a specific bit of information that will help you make a wise choice.

Trust in the spiritual process. When you approach it in honesty and openness, you are giving yourself the tools to make a good decision.

Trust that what you decide will help you live out a mission that expresses and fulfills your purpose on Earth.

Today's Spiritual Guideline

Having carefully considered the pros and cons of this decision making process, commit to spending an entire day immersed in your spiritual practice.

If possible, spend at least three hours of this day in silence; an entire day of silence is even better.

At the conclusion of the day, ask yourself, in all honesty, what you think you should do. Take into account all the wisdom that has been offered you through this journey, wisdom that has come from outside yourself as well as what you have learned though your spiritual practice and your thoughtful writings in your journal.

Above all, trust in your ability to decide. You can make the decision you know is good for you at this time. You can make a commitment to yourself to accept the decision that has emerged from this spiritually-based process.

Write a letter to yourself in your journal, committing to follow through with whatever decision you make. In the letter, confess and accept your feelings, both positive and negative, about this decision.

82 *The Negotiation*

You may have heard that the ideal negotiation is called a "win-win." That is, to be a truly satisfactory negotiation, both parties in the negotiation must have their real needs met; both must come away satisfied.

The first question you need to answer before entering into a meaningful negotiation is this: What are my real needs?

Well, most of us would like to have more money and experience greater material prosperity. And we'd probably like to live in a pleasant geographical location, with all the amenities, a low crime rate, and so on. But these are generic needs. It is important to also get in touch with those needs that are unique to you as an individual.

For example, there's the question of money, usually a topic of major concern in any job negotiation. How much is enough? How much do you need to accomplish all that you had in mind? More importantly, what amount of money will enable you to continue along the path of your sacred purpose?

Rely on your spiritual practice in this matter as you have in so many others. You have identified a sense of purpose. You have identified a potential job that will enable you to fulfill that purpose. Now it is important to ask yourself, *"What do I need to perform my mission?"*

Give yourself enough space, time, and quiet in which to identify your legitimate and real needs.

As in so much of this spiritual work, the answers may not come directly out of your meditations. Rather, you may receive guidance to seek out the opinions of others: a spouse, a close friend, a professional associate, a minister, or a spiritual guide. Consider carefully all the wisdom you receive, and in the quiet of your inner being, permit it to coalesce.

Once you have established your needs, these are what you must negotiate for as you speak with your potential employer. You may use whatever negotiation technique you choose, but always keep your purpose before you. Then you can negotiate accurately for yourself and for those whom you are called to serve.

Today's Spiritual Guideline

Spend some time considering the nature of your true needs. Thoughtfully record these in your journal.

Consider how you will negotiate for these needs. You may find it helpful to select a book, audio- or video tapes on the subject of negotiation. There are many excellent reference books available; I particularly recommend the book authored by Herb Cohen listed in the Bibliography.

Arrange with a friend, mentor, or coach for an opportunity to practice some of these negotiation techniques.

83 *Receiving*

I received what I worked so hard for,
and I give thanks.

Yet it crosses my mind to wonder,
did I get what I really wanted,
what I really needed?
(As they say, "Be careful what you ask for. You might get it.")

Fundamentally, I trust
there is a sacred reason I came into this world,
a purpose for which I am here.

I have been grounding myself in a spiritual practice
throughout the course of this journey.
Through my openness to the natural flow of life,
to the lessons I have so freely and lovingly been given, and
to the people who have been sent to me
when I needed them the most,
I have seen that I am fundamentally connected to all.

I am filled with hope and gratitude.
The larger Journey stretches out ahead.
And so, still cautious in the face of ambiguity,
but with great anticipation in the face of new opportunity,
I look forward to the challenges,
to the joy of life,
to the sense of purpose revealed
in this new mission now before me.

And I give thanks.

Today's Spiritual Guideline

Write a closing chapter in your journal. Consider:

- What have you learned?
- How has your life changed?
- What spiritual practices do you want to continue?
- What can you share with others to help them on the journey?

Give this journal a special place on your bookshelf.

As you begin your new job, you might want to begin another journal . . . new lessons await.

Epilogue

Just prior to completing this book, I spent several days in the Grand Canyon, hiking, camping, and rafting down the Colorado River.

The trip was not at all what I expected or planned. A few years ago, in my more couch-potato-like days, I would not even have considered such a trip. The thought of walking almost ten miles into one of the most yawning chasms on earth would have sent waves of fear through me.

Yet, there was an inner quiet voice urging me to take this trip, to move beyond my fears. I trusted the inner reassurance that I would be safe and cared for.

The experience was exhilarating and deeply spiritual. The first night, while stretching out on the canyon floor, I stared up into the full glory of the Milky Way Galaxy. I shivered as goose bumps formed on my skin, as I got a strong sense of both my insignificance and my fundamental interconnectedness with all of creation. I thought of my family, my friends, my little boy who had gone off on a journey that I will someday surely take as well. I realized that the fear I had felt those years ago in Williamsburg had been lifted. I knew I was in the right place.

I will ever be grateful for this voyage into spiritual depths I only barely suspected existed.

When I allow myself to flow with the Universe, to let it take me where I need to go, I experience joy and fulfillment far beyond what I think is possible.

These are the gifts of meaning that are freely offered to us all. May they be yours today and every day of your life.

Bibliography

Bolles, Richard Nelson. *What Color Is Your Parachute?* Berkeley, California: Ten Speed Press, reissued annually.

> This has been a classic book on job search and career development since 1971. Reissued and updated every year, Bolles takes the job seeker through a full course of assessment, planning, and networking exercises, not to mention the listing of tons of resources and ideas. Highly recommended by just about everyone in the field.

Cohen, Herb. *You Can Negotiate Anything*. New York: Bantam Books, 1982.

> A classic text still as fresh as the day it was published. Learn the concept of "win-win" and how to put it into practice to the benefit of you and all with whom you negotiate. Cohen makes a passionate argument for ethics, morality, and a grounding in fairness in all of our dealings. This is a very entertaining book as well.

Dyer, Wayne. *Manifest Your Destiny*. New York: HarperCollins, 1997.
_____ . *Your Sacred Self*. New York: HarperCollins, 1995.

> The popular psychologist of the seventies and eighties has brought it all home in the nineties by inviting us to get in touch with our essential, spiritual dimension. Two excellent works for becoming more firmly grounded in the "really real," or spiritual side of our existence. Useful as adjuncts to your spiritual practice.

Parker, Yana. *The Damn Good Résumé Guide*. Berkeley, California: Ten Speed Press, 1996.

> Parker probes into the making of an effective résumé, particularly the type known as a "functional résumé." As an old human resources manager, I have a certain bias toward the chronological format, but Parker offers some interesting, effective, and creative alternatives that can give you the opportunity to fully express your vision of mission and purpose to potential employers.

Sinetar, Marsha. *Do What You Love, The Money Will Follow*. New York: Dell Trade Paperbacks, 1987.

> An excellent "think" piece by a spiritually-grounded leader in career counseling. A useful adjunct and tool for use with your own spiritual practice. What Sinetar has written can be of assistance in your lifelong quest.

Zukav, Gary. *The Seat of the Soul*. New York: Fireside Books, 1990.

> Another work on spirituality and our fundamental interconnectedness. Read it very slowly and allow the full meaning to permeate your life. A very rewarding experience.

Photograph by Jessica Musgrove

About the Author

William Carver began his career in the early 1970s by studying for the Roman Catholic priesthood. Over the last twenty-five years, he has lived out his purpose through a variety of missions, including human resources director, consultant, personnel analyst, teacher, author, prison and hospital chaplain, factory worker, radio newscaster, and groundskeeper. He is now a human resources consultant with a diverse background in career and human resources management.

Carver spends much of his time speaking to people individually and in groups about effective and satisfying career development within the framework of the spiritual life. He is a graduate of St. Mary's Seminary and University, Baltimore, and Michigan State University.

While writing this book, he lived in the Tampa Bay area with his wife and two daughters and a wandering armadillo named Frank. He has since returned to his home state and now resides with his family in Franklin, Tennessee.